How to Get to the Top . . .
and Stay There

HOW TO GET TO THE TOP...

and stay there

Robert J. McKain

a Division of
American Management Associations

Library of Congress Cataloging in Publication Data

McKain, Robert J
  How to get to the top . . . and stay there.
  "A sequel to [the author's] Realize your potential, published
. . . 1975."
  Includes index.
  1. Success. I. Title.
HF5386.M195   650.1   80-67964
ISBN 0-8144-5653-7

©1981 AMACOM
A division of American Management Associations, New York.
All rights reserved. Printed in the United States of America.

This publication may not be reproduced, stored in a retrieval
system, or transmitted in whole or in part, in any form or by
any means, electronic, mechanical, photocopying, recording, or
otherwise, without the prior written permission of AMACOM,
135 West 50th Street, New York, N.Y. 10020.

First Printing

*Isn't it strange
That princes and kings
And clowns that caper
In sawdust rings
And common people
Like you and me
Are builders for eternity?*

*Each is given a bag of tools
A shapeless mass
A book of rules
And each must make
Ere life has flown
A stumbling block
Or a steppingstone.*

Acknowledgments

I owe a special debt of thanks to the following people:

To *Jack Collett*, whose considerable organizational talents were so helpful in structuring this book.

To *Jay Hulmes*, whose delightful cartoons are sprinkled throughout the text.

To *Louise Marinis*, who edited the manuscript and who showed extraordinary ability, perceptiveness, and patience.

And, especially, to my wife, *Juanita*, for her help and encouragement over a long period of time.

Preface

How to Get to the Top is a sequel to *Realize Your Potential*, published by AMACOM in 1975. This new book is a guide—a workbook, a blueprint—for personal growth and development. Do you want to be a better student or have a more rewarding life? Do you want to climb Mount Everest and be number one in your career? Or do you seek to conquer a more gentle slope, a smaller mountain? The choice is yours—it's your life. But getting to the top means personal fulfillment no matter what the climb. Your goal is to make the journey a happy one, to find peace of mind and enjoyment with others, to grow as a person, and to be productive.

The search for fulfillment continues throughout life, and the road is not always easy. How wonderful it would be if:

Kids didn't use drugs.
Marriages didn't break up.
Inflation didn't ravage savings.
People didn't get laid off or fired.
Serious diseases didn't strike children and adults.

But these things and more do happen, and if your climb to the top is to be worthwhile you need to be prepared to handle as many of these crises as possible.

There are vital personal reasons for sorting out your options, for examining the alternatives available to you in planning your work, your finances, your life. It's vital that you "protect your flank" and manage yourself by objectives. The aim of this book is to give you the frame of reference and the techniques you need for strategic life planning—techniques that you can easily master and use all your life.

You will be reading about tested techniques to:

Develop a healthy self-image.
Set and implement goals.
Control unhealthy stress.

Create your own "sizzle" in life.
Make more money.
Control your time.
Balance your priorities.

Getting to the top does not mean being super organized, super busy, or super tense. While some people are highly structured, others prefer spontaneity. None of the techniques described should be used inflexibly, nor should they detract from your personal independence. You're the judge and jury as to what you can or should use, so pick only those ideas and exercises that interest you.

In their simplicity these techniques may be deceptive. They can be used to build an elementary structure or a complex life plan. In the same way, the basic notes in the musical scale can be used to play anything from Chopsticks to Chopin. But getting a harmonious composition together, either in music or in life, represents one of the highest and most artistic forms of human expression.

As we grow, our lives should become richer and more meaningful, with greater personal rewards and peace of mind. Hermann Hesse has written that when we move from potential to deed, from possibility to realization, we become "true beings." The achievement of personal goals remains the only realistic path to success and fulfillment.

Many friends and associates were indirectly responsible for this book. Some have reached great heights in their business careers and in their personal lives, others have reached smaller but just as rewarding peaks. They are living proof that the techniques of getting to the top are available to everyone, but that the art of living lies in using them effectively. This is their story as I perceive it.

—Robert J. McKain

Contents

Section I	**The Process of Realizing Potential**	
	1. First Steps in Realizing Potential	3
	2. Coordinating Your Assets	8
Section II	**Checkpoint 1: Your Positive Mental Attitude**	
	3. Your Purpose in Life	17
	4. Dealing with Negativism	26
	5. Positive Mental Attitude and Stress	37
Section III	**Checkpoint 2: Your Goals**	
	6. The Nature of Goals	63
	7. Goal Setting	72
	8. Visualizing Success	80
Section IV	**Checkpoint 3: Your Self-Image**	
	9. The Nature of Your Self-Image	95
	10. Building Your Self-Image	104
	11. Reinforcing Your Self-Image	112
	12. Your Interpersonal Skills	125
Section V	**Checkpoint 4: Your Productivity**	
	13. Your Commitment	139
	14. Your Use of Time	149
	15. Your Use of Energy	161
Section VI	**Strategic Life Planning**	
	16. Building Your Life Strategy	173
	17. Creating an Action Plan	191
	Index	205

SECTION I

The Process of Realizing Potential

Live your life each day as you would climb mountains. An occasional glance toward the summit puts the goal in mind. Many beautiful scenes can be observed from each new vantage point. Climb steadily, slowly, enjoy each passing moment; and the view from the summit will serve as a fitting climax to the journey.

—Harold V. Melchert

1. First Steps in Realizing Potential

The very fact that you are reading this book should tell you something about yourself: you want to improve your life in some way. It may be that you feel your life can be more rewarding, or that you feel you can gain more recognition, or just that in spite of your achievements you feel that you can do even more. You *know*—deep inside—that you possess the potential for a better, more enjoyable life.

Can you achieve these things? You bet you can. In their book *Born to Win*, Muriel James and Dorothy Jongeward point out that all of us are born with what it takes to win at life.

Keep reading. In this book, you'll find exercises and activities that will enable you to shine some light on the real you, the one that lies waiting to be "actualized." If the most important tasks are to *know* yourself and to *be* yourself, then you must realize your own uniqueness and appreciate the uniqueness of others.

Climb Your Own Mountain

Arnold Burns is a garment industry executive in the play *A Thousand Clowns*. To some people, he is the epitome of mediocrity. But Arnold doesn't see himself that way. "You don't respect me very much," he tells his brother, the unhappy intellectual. "You want to be a hero, and I'm willing to deal with the available world. I'm not an exceptional man and I have a talent for surrender. I'm at peace. I'm not one of the bad guys. I take pride." And then he says, *"I'm the best possible Arnold Burns."*

Arnold Burns has climbed to the top of his own mountain. His message is clear: climb your mountain. You fail when you

lack purpose in life. The warning: don't try to climb someone else's mountain! You fail when your goals are false, vague, or unrealistic. And you fail when you lack a way to get where you want to go.

All of us have a mountain to climb, and although the terrain is largely determined by society, our family, and our work, we have much within ourselves to call upon to shape and define the mountain we want to climb. The top of the mountain is often foggy, but it is ours, whether imposed or self-created. Some people find the road up overwhelming; others find it challenging and fulfilling. People who have a clear, positive view are the ones who will get to the top and release their potential.

The issue is clear: your mountain is special, different from anyone else's. In order to climb it, you must:

1. Be realistic about how high you want to climb. Don't aim too far above "see" level if you want to avoid frustration.
2. Make a plan. Watch the crevices, avoid possible slides, and chart your most practicable course.
3. Bring all the useful tools you can get. The climb may be tougher than you think.
4. Climb with a partner. Remember—people need people, and aloneness means loneliness. Moreover, giving help to others and getting help from them is what provides life's greatest enrichment. Your mate, your family, your co-workers—all the people who form your personal universe—are important to you, and you are important to them.

Where Do You Start?

People have always searched for a better life, whether through religion, communes, and utopian settlements or through political extremes. With the discoveries of Freud, people began to look inside themselves, examining their most personal feelings and conflicts. The first steps in realizing your potential, then, are identifying, segregating, examining, and experiencing the most basic components of your makeup. To paraphrase Pogo, "I have met the enemy and he is me."

Quite often we must change our act because we are operating well below capacity and do not feel fulfilled. To make such a change may require improved skills, new habits, and life planning. You must work it out for yourself. You must discover who you are, and what feels best for you. You must look inside yourself and "write your own song."

> *You cannot teach a man anything. You can only help him discover it within himself.*
> —Galileo

Psychologists have pointed out that each of us has our own "norm" of performance. Your norm is consistent with your self-image, and you tend to perform steadily at that norm. If you see yourself as performing poorly in a given activity, you will probably approach the problem with a subconscious compromise: you will succeed, but not too well. You will set a ceiling for yourself that will allow you to go just about as high as is consistent with your self-image.

The only really effective antidote for unrealistic beliefs that limit you in realizing your full potential is to learn the truth about yourself. The business world spends tens of millions of dollars each year trying to help employees break free of their poor self-images by developing new beliefs about themselves. If a person's self-image improves and results in improved performance, both the employer and the employee win. Seminars, motivational programs, and contests are but a few of the methods used to help improve performance.

Realistically, for better or worse, your own norm, your own self-image is *you*. If you suspect that your present self-image is warped in some way, then you must learn the truth about yourself and reshape your self-image accordingly. That's a tough job, but there isn't a shred of doubt about whether it's worthwhile.

In a 1958 motivational research study Abraham Zalesnik of

Harvard University found that personal motivation, or the desire to achieve, does not need to be instilled in a person. It needs only to be released and given an opportunity to express itself. Dr. Zaleznik believes that this powerful force is "frozen" in a great many people. Unfreezing your innately strong will to achieve is what this book is all about. It makes no difference whether you are a student or a homemaker, working or retired; if you can remove the things that inhibit you, that mask your true worth as a person, you will have a more productive, more enjoyable life.

The Known and the Unknown

There are two kinds of potential. The first is *identified but unused* potential. This kind of potential is found in a specific skill or activity, and you know it well enough to measure it. For example, if your score for a particular activity is 7 on a scale of 0 to 10, with 10 as your full potential, there is obviously a gap between what you are doing and what you could be doing. This gap may be of your own choosing, or it may exist because of personal or job difficulties that you have been unable to surmount. In any case, you are aware of this unused potential, and your awareness means that you can go to work on closing the gap.

> *I am always longing to be with people more excellent than myself.*
> —Charles Lamb

The second kind of potential is *unidentified, unrecognized* potential. Such potential can lie fallow for a lifetime. Grandma Moses is an example. Fortunately, in her case the unidentified potential eventually surfaced. She was 79 years old when she discovered her latent painting ability, unused throughout her long life.

Discovering your unknown potential can help you develop new levels of competence and productivity and increase your enjoyment of life. The four-minute mile was a dream until Roger Bannister achieved it. It then became a standard for all good runners.

Awareness that potential exists is the first step toward realizing it, and age has nothing to do with the problem. You're never too young or too old. Golda Meir was 71 years old when she became prime minister of Israel. William Pitt was 24 when he became prime minister of Great Britain. George Bernard Shaw was 94 when one of his plays was first produced. Mozart was 7 when his first composition was published. Benjamin Franklin was a newspaper columnist at 16 and a framer of the Constitution at 81.

Some people dubbed the 1970s as the "me decade." It was meant pejoratively, but it referred to something meaningful. It signified the growing realization that we must look within ourselves for the satisfactions that have eluded us. The phenomenal success of the book *Jonathan Livingston Seagull* is a reflection of the interest people have in personal achievement. It is a story of growth, of rebellion against the confinement of small expectations. Jonathan wanted to be free, to soar, to fly as no gull had flown before. He wanted to find out just how high and how far he could go, and he worked at it every single day until he found out. He wanted to realize his full potential. Why the enormous interest in this story? Obviously no one wants to be an ordinary bird. We all want to soar.

2. Coordinating Your Assets

The word "coordination" is used throughout this book. Why? Because all the elements that go into realizing potential are constantly interacting and must be coordinated. I think a good way to describe this phenomenon is to draw an analogy with the field of estate planning, where coordination of assets is fundamental and works very clearly.

Back in the 1930s Stuart F. Smith, a brilliant executive, and Dr. Solomon Huebner, the famed teacher at the Wharton School of the University of Pennsylvania, were separately pioneering the now universally accepted procedure of coordinating a person's assets into a single plan for later disposition. The idea was to consider who owned the property, the amount and type of each asset, the instruments to distribute it (a will, deed, insurance agreements, business agreements), and the tax implications. All these complex factors would be considered in light of the family's goals. For the first time, this concept brought together the client's attorney, accountant, trust officer, and life insurance agent. Each of these people brought his or her special skills to the client's problems; they all worked as a team to find the best possible arrangement.

In the case of estate planning, it's easy to see that each asset and the legal instrument to distribute it is affected by all the other assets. The best results will never be achieved unless these assets are coordinated in a unified plan.

The diagram labeled "Your Financial Assets" shows this very well. For example, if you are making up a will and don't consider your jointly owned property (which doesn't pass under your will) or your life insurance or company group or pension plans (which also don't ordinarily pass under a will), your estate may end up paying a great deal more in taxes than necessary. In other words, if you don't coordinate your financial assets, Uncle Sam will do it his way—which usually means 20, 30, or 50 percent more in taxes. So thoughtful people get a list of all

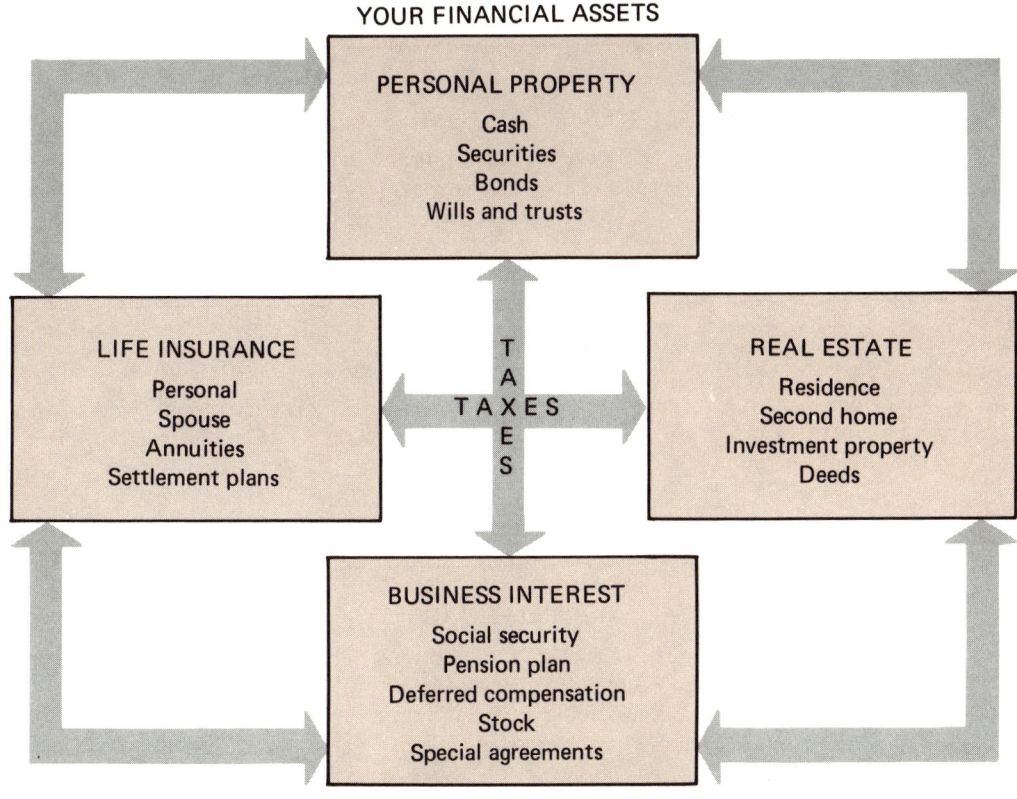

their assets and liabilities and decide what their goals are. They then get the help they need to achieve their objectives and to pay as little tax as possible. That's what coordination in estate planning is all about.

Now let's take that same diagram and relabel it "Your Personal Assets." As the chart suggests, your personal asset structure consists of four critical, interdependent elements that must be coordinated. In this book, we will be talking about these four elements very specifically and very personally: your positive mental attitude, your goals, your self-image, and your productivity. In financial planning losses due to lack of coordination are measured in dollar bills, but in personal planning losses are measured by stress, career setbacks, personal and marital difficulties, and lack of fulfillment.

Let's see how these four personal assets relate to each other. Suppose you are unable to achieve a specific goal. The problem

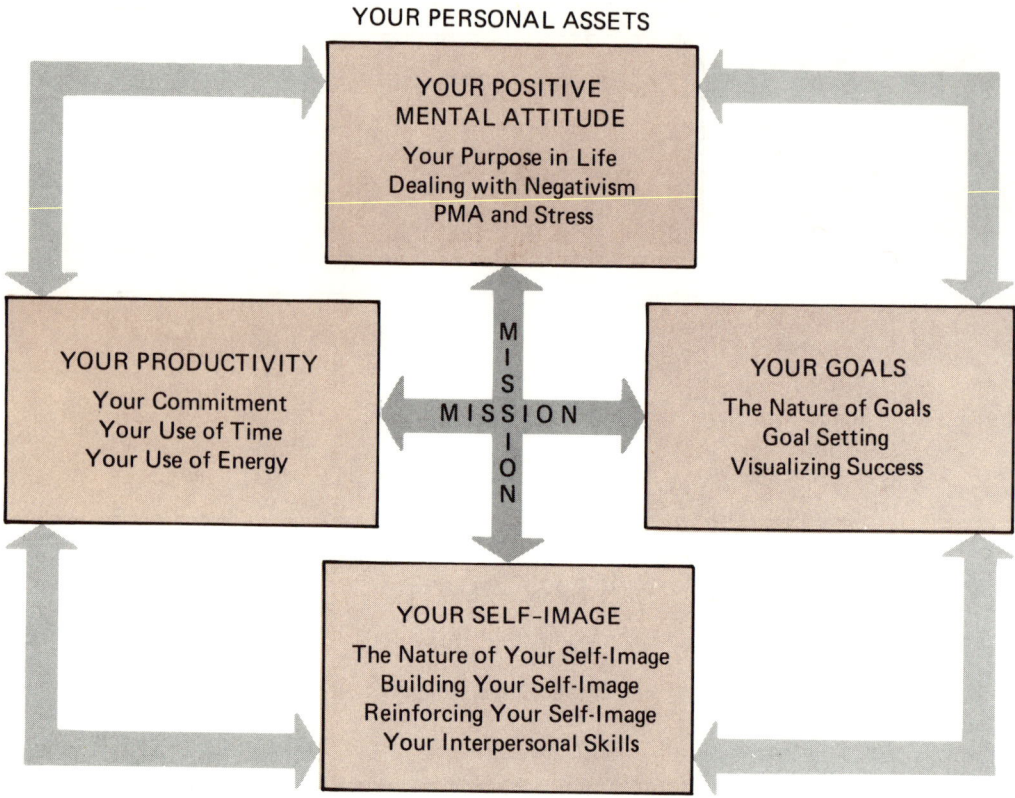

may be due to personal difficulties (a self-image problem) or to job difficulties (a productivity problem). On the other hand, the goal may be poorly defined. If you can redefine the goal, you may find that your mental image becomes much more positive. There is also the possibility that the goal is not achievable because of special circumstances in your life. You must examine the situation to determine whether you are blaming yourself for something that is beyond your control or whether you are

No two human beings have made, or ever will make, exactly the same journey in life.

—Sir Arthur Keith

> A. J. Cronin, author of *Keys of the Kingdom, The Citadel,* and many other works, said that when he started his first novel he found it difficult to express himself. "A sudden desolation struck me like an avalanche. I decided to abandon the whole thing." Cronin threw away his manuscript. A friend got him to dig his papers out of the trash can, and in three months of what Cronin called "ferocious effort," he finished *Hatter's Castle.* The rest is history.

blaming others when your own shortcomings are the stumbling block.

These four "checkpoints of potential"—positive mental attitude, goals, self-image, and productivity—must be integrated with all aspects of your life: your career, family, health, financial, spiritual, and leisure goals. All work in tandem, and all are coordinated by your sense of mission in life. Make them work for you by synchronizing them, and make sure they aren't at cross-purposes.

The ideas and exercises in this book are not difficult to follow or understand, but they are difficult to apply. You need determination and persistence. Don't be discouraged. We are going through four checkpoints, and our goal is a coordinated life plan for you.

The Checkpoints of Potential

Checkpoint 1: Your Positive Mental Attitude (PMA). Your ability to hold firm to a positive attitude is what sustains your commitment through thick and thin. The specific components are:

1. A philosophy of success and a sound life purpose.
2. An ability to cope with negativism.
3. A positive response to stress.

Checkpoint 2: Your Goals. Goals are the focus of your commitment and give your life purpose. Here we consider:

1. Making goals realistic and challenging.
2. Setting goals that work.
3. Building the meaning of goals.

Well-defined goals lead to successful activity and energize the human system.

Checkpoint 3: Your Self-Image.   In this section you will take a deep look inside, at your:

1. Self-image.
2. Self-evaluation.
3. Self-acceptance.

If you don't develop a strong, positive self-image, you'll blow the whole ballgame!

Checkpoint 4: Your Productivity.   The factors discussed in this section are especially relevant to people who are career-oriented:

1. Your personal commitment.
2. Your use of time.
3. Your energy level.

How you handle these things determines your personal thermostat, which in turn determines your level of activity. And, as you'll discover later, successful activity is a key to the full realization of your potential.

You work with these checkpoints every day, consciously or unconsciously. Working with them separately is not difficult—it is their interaction that sometimes causes trouble. In the final section, we'll tie it all together so that you can develop your own coordinated life plan.

What Can the Use of Potential Mean to You?

The effective coordination of the checkpoints of potential has a cumulative effect. Outstanding people in the fields of music, art, medicine, and business have tremendous reserves of energy, and many of them have lived unusually long and rewarding lives. Their capacity to achieve and to enjoy their lives bears little relation to accumulating money. Their enjoyment rests on fulfilling their potential in whatever special areas they have chosen. This triggers their potential in all other areas of their lives. They enjoy their work, and they are very good at it. They enjoy living—and are very good at it.

> *A man's life, like a piece of tapestry, is made up of many strands which interwoven make a pattern. To separate a single one and look at it alone, not only destroys the whole, but gives the strand itself a false value.*
>
> —Learned Hand

Using This Book

The purpose of this book is to help you realize your potential. It has been organized as a workbook, with practical exercises throughout. I believe that this format helps you see the effort as a *process*. You will move from section to section, making notes along the way (there is ample space on the pages), always moving through self-analysis. Keep a pencil handy and use it to do the exercises, jot down thoughts as they occur, or note ideas for your attention at another time. Underline the portions that give you some special, vivid insight. Don't try to get through the book in one sitting. One section at a time is probably best. Move at your own pace.

Throughout the book I have tried to give you the tools you need to achieve all that you can. Like all tools, however, the measure of their worth depends on how they are applied. They must be used well to do the proper job.

As you read, you will be measuring your potential in various exercises on a scale of 0 to 10, ranging from nonuse to full use. This will be a "judgment call" on your part and you should base your scores on your personal feelings. For example, a score of 8 would indicate that you are highly satisfied with your performance in a given area but still feel you are short of perfection. A score of 5 would indicate lesser satisfaction.

Quantifying your potential will change the way you feel about yourself and your work. More important, it will show you, with reasonable accuracy, your ability to grow further in every aspect of your life.

The process is simple and workable. It is, I hope, no more

complicated than the ship captain who intrigued his crew for years. Every morning he opened his safe, took out a slip of paper, read it silently, and then returned it to the safe. When he died, the crew could not wait to see what was in the safe. The officer in charge opened the safe in front of the assembled crew and read the slip:

Starboard right, port left.

SECTION II

Checkpoint 1: Your Positive Mental Attitude

No man ever sank under the burdens of the day. It's when tomorrow's burden is added to the burden of today that the road is more than a man can bear.

—George McDonald

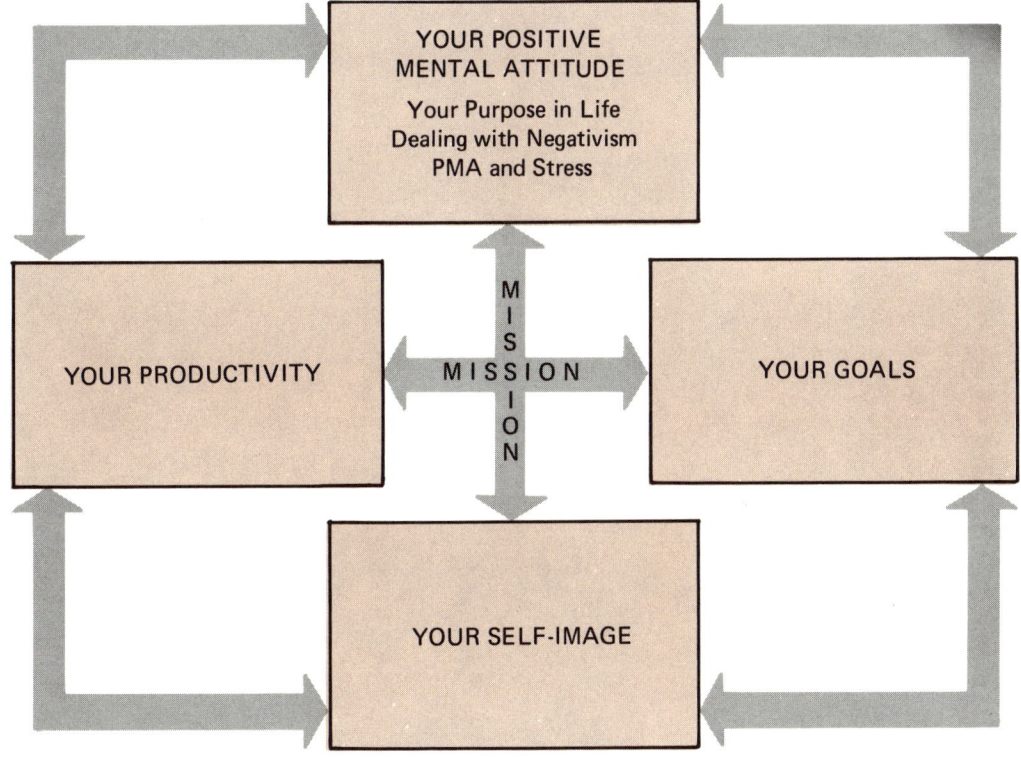

3. Your Purpose in Life

These days there are many books dealing with the changes we face as we pass through the various decades of our lives. Each decade has its own problems and opportunities, accompanied by its own peculiar physical and mental changes. Maintaining our physical and mental health as we pass through these periods demands that we be highly adaptable to the oncoming changes. Here are a few tips that can help you weather the storms:

Know who you really are. Know your assets—your faith, values, and strengths.

Make a commitment to develop your worth and dignity as a person and to share your growth with others. Consider this your moral responsibility.

Know that your greatest treasure is your self-image. You must have a good opinion of yourself. You may respect the goals and advice of others, but you must be the master of your own destiny.

Live in the present. The past is over. Remembering the painful past is part of your learning experience, but you shouldn't dwell on it. Today and tomorrow are infinitely more important than yesterday.

See yourself at your best. Practice pride and confidence each day. Replace your worries with positive thinking and work toward your present goal. Your strong points are the real you—your weak points are simply obstacles to be overcome. Visualize yourself as a success in your desired field.

Developing and Sustaining a Positive Mental Attitude

Your positive mental attitude (PMA) is one of your most basic assets in realizing your potential. It is vital to your physical and mental health—your overall well-being. The truth is that when you experience confidence, happiness, and success, you enjoy life. When you suffer from such negative feelings as anxiety, fear, frustration, worry, and self-condemnation, life is a drag. It's as simple as that.

While the effects of negativism can be easily identified, the cure for negativism is elusive. One of the reasons is that "positive thinking" is often used to solve only temporary crises. ("I will get that job." "I will be more relaxed and self-confident at the staff meeting.") Positive thinking in such instances is being used as a superficial solution to a deep-seated problem. In fact, it is almost impossible to think positively about a given situation if you have a negative self-image and are not using your time, energy, and goals effectively to support a positive mental attitude.

Here are some thoughts on how to generate and sustain a positive mental attitude:

Don't sell yourself short. Undoubtedly, you have much to be proud of. Identify your strengths and use them to your best advantage in your career and your social life.

Make your growth work for you. You are engineered for happiness, excellence, and success. Once you get your PMA going for you, it is like money in the bank—it's compounded daily and grows in value.

Get excited about your possibilities. Think about them, dream about them. Write down what specific changes in your life might mean to you.

Don't force your solutions. You will be developing strategies later in the book. As you begin to implement them, let the process happen naturally.

Defining a Purpose or Mission

Defining a purpose or a mission for your life can provide the answers to some basic questions: "What must I live up to? What are my obligations? To what must I commit myself? What should my goals be? How can I get the greatest satisfaction out of my life?" People differ in their goals, lifestyles, thought processes, convictions, and natural talents, and whatever *you* define as *your* purpose should be special and valuable. It should provide you with a reason for living and the basis for a positive mental attitude.

Once you fully experience the rewards and satisfaction that come through successful activity, you become aware of what you can and must do. Through your growth, you sense the exhilaration of being a complete person—you "lose" yourself in success. That doesn't mean you lose control of yourself or the direction your life is to take. It means that you shift focus from yourself ("How did I do? What did they think of me? Did my nervousness show?") to the experience itself and concentrate on the objective events ("Did my plans work? What contingencies could I have anticipated? What lessons are to be learned?").

We are all familiar with the inventor who stays up all night trying to get a bug out of an idea, the lawyer who pores over the evidence until morning looking for a breakthrough, the teacher who works with a student to explain an obscure point after everyone else has gone home. The sense of satisfaction gained from seeing such problems through cannot be equaled. These are the occasions when we lose ourselves, when we are in overdrive, which is effortless and gives us a real "high."

What Purpose Means to Your Life

Dr. Hans Selye is an outstanding authority on stress. He writes that the individual's ultimate aim in life is "to express himself as fully as possible, according to his own lights, and to achieve a sense of security.... Within the limits set by our innate abilities, we should strive for excellence, for the best we can do."* You may wonder what that has to do with stress. Think about it, and you'll see that without the sense of purpose he describes, we are filled with stress over our *failure* to move our life forward. Think also about some of the best-known people in history—you know their names through their achievements. If Michelangelo had just dreamed about the Last Judgment instead of going through the terrible difficulties he endured to get the painting on the ceiling of the Sistine Chapel, you might never have heard of him. If Artur Rubenstein had only thought about how nice it would be to play the piano instead of working every day for an entire lifetime, he might have been an unknown. If Albert Schweitzer had gone on playing the organ for

---

Stress Without Distress (Philadelphia: J. B. Lippincott, 1974).

pleasure and not actually built and operated his hospital in Lambaréné, scholars of Bach would be the only ones to know him through a book he wrote on Bach's music.

The list could go on for pages and pages. You know these people because they had a deep, abiding purpose in life, dedicated themselves to that purpose, and worked until they accomplished at least a substantial part of what they dreamed of doing.

A generation ago, Albert M. Gray of the Prudential Life Insurance Company traveled throughout the country delivering a vital message about successful habits and purpose in life. He said this about a worthwhile purpose:

> *Any resolution or decision you make is simply a promise to yourself which isn't worth a tinker's damn until you have formed the habit of making it and keeping it. Here's what happens. Your resolution or decision has become a habit, and you don't have to make it on this particular morning.*
>
> *And the reason for your seeming like a different man living in a different world lies in the fact that for the first time in your life, you have become master of yourself and master of your likes and dislikes by surrendering to your purpose in life. That is why behind every success there must be a purpose and that is what makes purpose so important to your future....*
>
> *First of all, your purpose must be practical and not visionary. But in making your purpose practical, be careful not to make it logical. Make it a purpose of the sentimental or emotional type. Remember that needs are logical, while wants and desires are sentimental and emotional. Your needs will push you just so far, but when your needs are satisfied, they will stop pushing you. If, however, your purpose is in terms of wants or desires, then your wants and desires will keep pushing you long after your needs are satisfied and until your wants and desires are fulfilled.*
>
> *You won't have to be told how to find your purpose or how to identify it or how to surrender to it. If it's a big purpose, you will be big in its accomplishment. If it's an unselfish purpose, you will be honest and honorable in the accomplishment of it. So be very careful of your identification of this purpose and in your surrender to it. It is going to make you form the habit of doing the things which failures do not like to do—and which you and I do not naturally like to do.*

Many men have said, "But I have a family to support and I have to make a living for my family and myself. Isn't that enough of a purpose?" No, it isn't a sufficiently strong purpose to make you form the habit of doing the things you don't like to do, for the very simple reason that it is easier to adjust to the hardships of a poor living than it is to adjust to the hardships of making a better one. All of which seems to prove that the strength which holds you to your purpose is not your own strength but the strength of the purpose itself.

If you grasp the significance of purpose, you can redirect your thinking and life planning so that your efforts will come together and shape your resolve. This book will help you.

Your Mission Statement

How you view your purpose in life is basic in determining your level of personal fulfillment. If your mission is not clear, it will be worth your time to think it through, to write it down, and to refine it so that it is personally meaningful to you. A well-thought-through mission statement provides the foundation needed to develop a coordinated life plan.

Your mission statement should describe what you are doing for other people and the service you perform for which you are paid. It should clarify why you're doing what you're doing and what benefits you provide to others. It sounds elementary, but it isn't. Remember that your key goals are based on how you view your mission. For example, an automobile manufacturer might state his mission in two ways:

To provide large, comfortable cars that will help people get to where they're going, at a reasonable profit to the company.

OR

To provide adequate transportation that will help people get to where they're going at the lowest possible cost and at a reasonable profit to the company.

There is no need to elaborate on the devastating impact the first mission statement has had on the automobile industry in the United States.

> "Life force" means growth. The very process is joyful. We sense it instinctively when we see a newborn child. Why don't we hold onto that joy through all the other stages of growth, right to the end?

Your purpose in life ties in with your goals, and your career mission and your personal mission may overlap. For example, a financial planner's mission statement might be: "Helping my family and myself move beyond economic hardships by helping other people solve their financial and estate problems."

■ *Exercise: Preparing a Mission Statement*

In your own words, draft a statement that expresses the purpose or mission of your life. Write freely, and don't put a limit on your thoughts at this time.

_____
_____
_____
_____
_____

■

> *Existence is a strange bargain. Life owes us little; we owe it everything. The only true happiness comes from squandering ourselves for a purpose.*
> —*John Mason Brown*

Hot Beliefs

The expression "hot beliefs" was first used by William James to describe the fervor that characterizes people who have deep, firm convictions in life—people who *believe* in themselves, their values, their goals. According to James, hot beliefs release new energy. They strengthen our will and inspire greater achievement than we thought ourselves capable of.

David McClelland, a highly respected educator and author of well-known studies on motivation, puts it another way. He says that people who have motivation and little desire for achievement need "ideological fervor" to stimulate them.

And Thomas J. Watson, Jr., legendary head of IBM, put it this way in a speech: "Belief and philosophy constitute a transcendent factor which outweighs technology, economic resources, or anything else in achieving success. All these things weigh heavily, but they are, I think, transcended by how strongly the people in the organization believe in its basic precepts and how faithfully they carry them out."

I long ago concluded that "hot beliefs" turn cold for two main reasons. First, we do not absorb into our bloodstream a philosophy of realizing potential. We need to understand that all human beings have very great psychological and emotional needs, which are built in. They can be broadly understood as the need for *self-respect*—which encompasses our confidence in ourselves to cope with life's problems, our desire for a better life, our enjoyment in accomplishing something—and the need for the *respect of others*, which encompasses recognition, approval, and acceptance from other people. We must recognize these needs and realize that they are justifiable. We need them to build a set of goals around their satisfaction, and to steep ourselves in a commitment to achieving those goals. If we can translate that commitment into action, we are "hot"!

The second reason hot beliefs turn cold is that we give up, or level out. We can't solve problems in a difficult time in our life and we don't know where to turn for help. It happens frequently in the business world, where men and women with great potential meet some reverses and then retreat instead of forging ahead. They can't get over the hump. What a pity to waste so much talent!

Putting It All Together

Arnold Toynbee said: "Apathy can only be overcome by enthusiasm, and enthusiasm can only be aroused by two things: first, an idea which takes the imagination by storm, and second a definite, intelligible plan for carrying that idea into practice!"

Make it your business to live a good life. Find and remove the shackles of distrust, fear, anger, apathy, and anxiety. Analyze the points in this book and find out what is holding you back from the kind of life you want—then do something about it. The days of your life are precious and few—you can't afford to waste any of them. Each day you withdraw from your life bank account is like a blank check. It's up to you to fill in the value with interest.

If getting on with your life can be likened to a voyage, we can say that your goals are your destination and your fuel is your mental attitude—you need a never-ending supply of PMA to take you farther and farther:

Concentrate on the rewards of success, not the penalties of failure.

Expect to win. You can be as strong as your faith.

Enthusiasm and optimism are your spark plugs. The key to

The Benefits of PMA

In his bestselling book, *Anatomy of an Illness,* Norman Cousins recounts his recovery from a connective tissue disease that was presumed by doctors to be fatal. Mr. Cousins did not accept the verdict. After reading *The Stress of Life* by Hans Selye, in which Selye explains the negative chemical changes caused by tension, frustration, and anger, Cousins reasoned that hope, laughter, faith, and confidence could just as easily cause positive chemical changes in his body. As a vital part of his recovery program, he secured the funniest films and books he could get. He found very quickly that ten minutes of belly laughter provided two hours of relief from severe pain. Ultimately, by using laughter and large injections of ascorbic acid, he was able to go completely off drugs and move on to recovery.

William James has said that human beings tend to live too far within self-imposed limits. Mr. Cousins clearly shows that the outer limits and benefits of a positive mental attitude are as yet barely explored.

> *A Doctor's Prescription for PMA*
>
> One evening in 1808 a gaunt, sad-faced man entered the offices of Dr. James Hamilton in Liverpool, England. The doctor asked:
>
> "Are you sick?"
>
> "Yes, doctor, sick of a mortal illness," said the man.
>
> "What illness?"
>
> "I am depressed by life. I can find no happiness anywhere, nothing amuses me, and I have nothing to live for. If you can't help me, I shall kill myself."
>
> "The malady is not fatal. You only need to get out of yourself. You need to laugh; to get some pleasure from life."
>
> "What shall I do?"
>
> "Go to the circus tonight to see Grimaldi, the clown. Grimaldi is the funniest man alive. He'll cure you."
>
> A spasm of pain crossed the poor man's face as he said: "Doctor, don't jest with me; I am Grimaldi."
>
> —John Summerfield Wimbish

maintaining them is to keep your plan for success workable and realistic. Failure is a downer.

Make sure you really care about your goals. If your sights are too low, you won't think it really matters whether you reach the goals. You've got to *want* to succeed.

■ Activity: Boost Your PMA

1. For the next 60 days, make a conscious, full commitment to your career, your company, and other people. Give everything you've got in the most positive way. The results may surprise you.
2. In your conversations use positive, encouraging words. Concentrate on upbeat adjectives and adverbs; use action verbs. Practice positive speech from morning to night.
3. Associate with optimistic, successful people. Talk about your good spirits and expectations, because that kind of thinking is contagious.
4. Feel good about yourself. Value what you are and what you have.
5. Let your fears rest in peace. Life presents us all with an array of problems, many of which we have little or no control over. Don't be obsessed with what might happen.

4. Dealing with Negativism

The capacity to be positive, to grow, and to stay young in spirit was well stated by General Douglas MacArthur:

Nobody grows old by merely living a number of years. People grow old by deserting their ideals. Years may wrinkle the skin, but to give up interest wrinkles the soul. Worry, doubt, self-distrust, fear, and despair—these are the long, long years that bow the head and turn the growing spirit back to dust. Whatever your years, there is in every being the love of wonder, the undaunted challenge of events, the unfailing appetite for what's next, and the joy in the game of life. You are as young as your ambition, as old as your doubt; as young as your self-confidence, as old as your fear; as young as your hope, as old as your despair.

Accept into your mind and soul those thoughts that are positive and that express your goals. Then build meaning into your system by concentrating, emphasizing, and developing these mental images.

The Power of Belief

The power of belief is not a myth. It is a reality. You will obtain what you think about most because you will direct your energy toward it—whether it is money, security, recognition, or learning a new skill.

Tex Colbert, Chrysler Corporation's dynamic former chairman, who ran an airplane engine plant during World War II, forcefully demonstrated the power of belief. When he assumed his new responsibility, he called his department heads together and said, "If I hear any of you say that this new engine and plane won't be built on time, won't fly, won't win the war, that it's the other fellow's fault, I will ask for your resignation. Our job is to win the war and that's what we're going to do." Tex Colbert's plant went on to win the highest production honors.

If you feel that your overall attitude is negative, remember that you can often change your attitude by changing your physical actions. Try smiling a lot more often than you habitually do. It's difficult to remain angry when you are smiling, and other people will find it hard to be angry with you.

Anxiety is quite possibly the most serious ailment in this country. We hold post-mortems on all our failed opportunities and our errors. We worry about the past and we worry about the future. One of the worst tragedies is that worry and negativism are contagious and are easily contracted by susceptible people, with devastating effect.

Develop a positive mental attitude and spread it around. Avoid negative people. When you must deal with a negative situation, try to look at it in a positive way. A dramatic example—under the most trying conditions—occurred during World War II when General Creighton Abrams and his men were totally surrounded. His reaction: "Gentlemen, for the first time in the history of this campaign we are now in a position to attack the enemy in any direction."

You've got to come to grips with the core of negativism and change your negative self-concept by means of personal growth. Once your negative self-image has been eradicated, you will find a host of other negatives disappearing.

In the book *Body, Mind, and Spirit*, Dr. Elwood Worcester relates the testimony of a world-famous scientist:

> *Up to my fiftieth year I was an unhappy, ineffective man. None of the works on which my reputation rested were published.... I lived in a constant sense of gloom and failure....*
>
> *I had read some of the literature of New Thought, which at the time appeared to be bunkum, and some statements of William James on the directing of attention to what is good and useful and ignoring the rest. One saying of his stuck in my mind: "We might have to give up our philosophy of evil, but what is that in comparison with gaining a life of goodness?" Hitherto these doctrines had seemed to me only mystical theories, but realizing that my soul was sick and growing worse and that my life was intolerable, I determined to put them to the proof.... I decided to limit the period of*

conscious effort to one month, as I thought this time long enough to prove its value or its worthlessness to me. During this month I resolved to impose certain restrictions on my thoughts. If I thought of the past, I would try to let my mind dwell only on its happy, pleasing incidents, the bright days of my childhood, the inspiration of my teachers and the slow revelation of my life work. In thinking of the present, I would deliberately turn my attention to its desirable elements—my home, the opportunities my solitude gave me to work, and so on—and I resolved to make the utmost use of these opportunities and to ignore the fact that they seemed to lead to nothing. In thinking of the future, I determined to regard every worthy and possible ambition as within my grasp. Ridiculous as this seemed at the time, in view of what has come to me since, I see that the only defect of my plan was that it aimed too low and did not include enough.

The scientist then tells how within one week he felt happier and better than ever before. He concludes:

As I look back over all these changes, it seems to me that in some blind way I stumbled on a path of life and set forces to working for me which before were against me.

Strengthening Positive Thoughts

As you begin to think more positively, it is important to collect positive thoughts. Emphasize the *frequency* of your positive thoughts, rather than their intensity. Here's what you do:

1. Be specific about the positive thoughts you'd like to cultivate. Write them down. Check the ones you'd like to strengthen.
2. Identify a specific stimulus, like the ringing of a telephone, eating, or water on your hands, that occurs early in the day and frequently.
3. Make a contract that when the stimulus occurs, you will think the positive thoughts you have written down—sort of like self-hypnosis.
4. Take action associated with the stimulus and the positive thought.

> A salesman—let's call him Jim—was often subject to depression because of being rejected by prospects when he called for appointments. Jim listed these positive thoughts: "This person needs my services; I feel excited, enthusiastic; and my voice conveys conviction, sincerity." Because he used the phone frequently, Jim picked the dial tone as his stimulus, or trigger. He made a contract with himself to think of one of the positive thoughts when he heard the dial tone just before he placed a call. After a few calls, Jim sensed that he was much more in charge of himself. He had made a small but important step toward successful activity.

Focusing on Key Activities

In today's culture we are presented with a bewildering array of options, and we often try to focus on too many things at once. Unfortunately, the tendency to waver between options without making a choice leads to frustration. Below is a well-known illustration used in psychology to demonstrate the principle of focusing. If you concentrate on the two outer, shaded segments of the drawing, you will see two human profiles facing each other. The white segment in the middle becomes the background. But if you concentrate on the white center, the shaded segments become the background and you see a vase. It is apparent that you can choose your focus.

■ Activity: Trigger Your Positive Thinking

Make it a habit to substitute pleasant, wholesome mental images for unpleasant "worry images."

Each time you find yourself starting to think negatively, use this as a *signal* to fill your mind immediately with pleasant mental pictures of the past or to anticipate pleasant future experiences. Negative thoughts thus become a "trigger" for practicing positive thinking. ■

■ Activity: Punch Up Your Act

To develop a positive stance try:

Smiling: You will make yourself feel more like smiling if you make yourself smile. A happy face can be self-perpetuating. But stay away from funerals.

Standing erect: You will make yourself feel better and more confident if you look confident and walk smartly—don't slump along as if life just isn't worth the trouble.

Listening to others: You will become more interesting to yourself and to others if you listen to and show interest in what other people have to say. Get out of your shell. ■

Because the ability to focus triggers the goal-oriented mind, it is essential that you understand what focusing means in terms of the coordination of your assets. Focusing implies a number of things: concentration, giving yourself to what you are doing, and being intensely involved in your job, an idea, your community, or your family. When you focus your camera, you bring two images together to form a sharp, clear picture. When you focus on strategic planning, you do much the same thing—you define and clarify your problems, your mission, and your goals. You produce clear, sharp pictures and then things begin to fall into place that previously seemed to defy solution. When you finally choose a focus and concentrate on a goal, you begin to use more fully your past experiences, resources, and talents. W. Timothy Gallwey, writing about concentration in his book *The Inner Game of Tennis*, says that concentration is not seeing the tennis ball as the racquet hits it; it is seeing the *seams* on the ball. Such intense concentration comes only when you have focused on something you love.

Focusing and Problem Solving

Today we face a bewildering array of international and national problems—the oil crisis, inflation, natural disasters, and so on. At the same time we are often overloaded with personal problems—family, career, finances, health. Sometimes it seems that the best course would be to leave town, to turn tail and run. This is the time when focusing becomes essential. Take one problem at a time, concentrate on that crisis only. If you try to consider all your problems at once, you end up in a muddle. By taking your problems one at a time, you gain the perspective needed to decide whether to meet the problem, defer it, or sidestep it entirely.

Focusing is an essential part of goal setting. Breaking a problem (or goal) down into smaller, do-able activities brings it into increasingly sharper focus so that you can deal effectively with it. Suppose, for example, that you are having marital problems. Using the graph covered in Chapter 17, you might break down the category of love as follows:

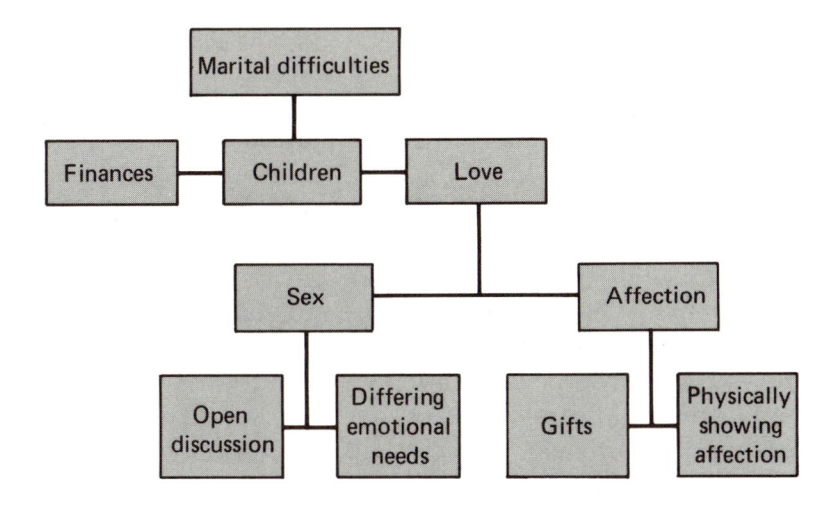

```
                    Marital difficulties
                           |
       Finances ── Children ── Love
                                |
                    Sex ─────── Affection
                   /   \         /      \
           Open   Differing   Gifts   Physically
        discussion emotional         showing
                    needs            affection
```

Dealing with marital problems can be very difficult, but it's no great shakes to begin to show affection through words and gestures, to bring a gift unexpectedly, or to remember an anniversary.

Focusing is the key to fulfillment and to finding meaning and purpose in life. When you focus on a project of vital interest to you, when you clearly define it, and when you enjoy the project and become good at it, you're on your way to the top of your mountain.

Career Burnout

Career counselors are increasingly identifying career burnout as a malady of the working world, but the same syndrome appears among people who are not necessarily in paid jobs—volunteers, homemakers, the self-employed, almost anyone in any field of activity. It usually sets in when a person begins questioning his or her personal worth. Quite simply, the person no longer feels that what he or she is doing is important. Stress, boredom, overwork, and dissatisfaction with the results all contribute to burnout and very often lead to alcoholism, depression, and other serious diseases.

Sometimes it's a matter of being in the wrong job or field. Arthur Miller dramatizes this effectively in his stage classic *Death of a Salesman.* Willie Loman's life was poisoned by his failure in a job that brought him few rewards and destroyed his family. Willie had a calling he could have pursued successfully: he loved to work with his hands. His masterpiece was the set of steps he had built at the front door of his house. But he was driven to a different life—the life of a salesman—and it killed him.

Career burnout doesn't necessarily mean that you should change careers. What it definitely does mean is that you should take a hard look at your present situation. Carefully evaluate where you are, where you *want* to go, and whether you are headed in the right direction. You need to stand back and gain some perspective, to take your eyes off the trees in your vicinity and see the whole forest. Get away from the scene of the action by removing yourself physically, if you can, perhaps using vacation time to be alone and do some real soul-searching.

You must evaluate your career realistically and decide whether it would be better to develop present opportunities or to seek a change. Assess your career history and your performance—are you miscast? If you are uncertain, consult with professionals. They can act as a sounding board and provide proper counseling. Indeed, career testing can uncover hidden skills and strengths that may be the key to your future happiness.

If you do decide to change careers, keep in mind this advice from an executive recruiter: "Even if you are burned out, I'd strongly advise you to put on a happy face at work. Be busy where you can accomplish things. You are going to market—like a used car. If the car is in good condition and it is bright and shining, it will sell. Most employers assume that if someone's unhappy where he or she is, it's going to carry over to the new job."

> *If you do a good job for others, you heal yourself at the same time, because a dose of joy is a spiritual cure. It transcends all barriers.*
> —Ed Sullivan

Career Indecisiveness

Even people with impressive job qualifications may fail to find fulfillment in their work. They fall far short of achieving their potential; they flounder. They wonder, "What's wrong with me?" On the surface, objective factors—need for more pay, annoyance with associates, failure to get choice assignments—

> The person who loves his work has more zest, eats better, sleeps better, and lives longer. He takes frustrations in stride, gets more done, and is more efficient! His positive mental attitude is constantly being reinforced by career success, and vice versa. Having the right career is the single most critical factor in realizing your potential. It is your backbone.
>
> An old Chinese proverb says:
> If you would be happy for one hour, take a nap.
> If you would be happy for a day, go fishing.
> If you would be happy for a week, kill a pig and eat it.
> If you would be happy for a month, get married.
> If you would be happy for a year, inherit a fortune.
> If you would be happy for life, love your work.

often seem to be the cause. But this is not usually the real problem, for a certain amount of dissatisfaction is part of almost any job.

The real problem for most of us is lack of clarity about what we want from our working life. And when we are indecisive about this core aspect, our dissatisfaction may interfere with all other aspects of our life. Because we aren't sure about what end results we desire, we start to hold ourselves in check. We don't apply our talents, we do not give of our time and abilities to others, we even hold back emotionally. We find then that our personal relationships suffer too. We have, in fact, put happiness on "hold."

Indecisiveness about your career may take over when you consciously decide that you want out of the rat race. Or it may be the result of a feeling that you don't measure up to your expectations of success. Whatever the cause, the result can be disastrous. It warps your self-image, which in turn affects your performance—on and off the job. Since your career is the dominating structure of your life, it has to be sturdy.

We will deal with stress in some detail in the next chapter, but the succession of problems triggered by negativism and indecisiveness is so dangerous that I have placed a diagram here to show just how far-reaching it is. Look at the drawing box by box and see how many of the trouble spots apply to you. Circle them, and draw lines to connect them. You will get a profile of yourself that may shed a lot of light for you.

Remember, there is no more important element in your self-development than your career. The satisfaction, enjoyment, and success you derive from your career support your positive self-

---

> Work is the foundation of all business, the source of all prosperity, and the parent of genius.
> Work can do more to advance youth than his own parents, be they ever so wealthy.
> It is represented in the humblest savings and has laid the foundation of every fortune.
> It is the salt that gives life its savor, but it must be loved before it can bestow its greatest blessing and achieve its greatest end.
> When loved, work makes life sweet, purposeful, and fruitful.
>
> Anonymous

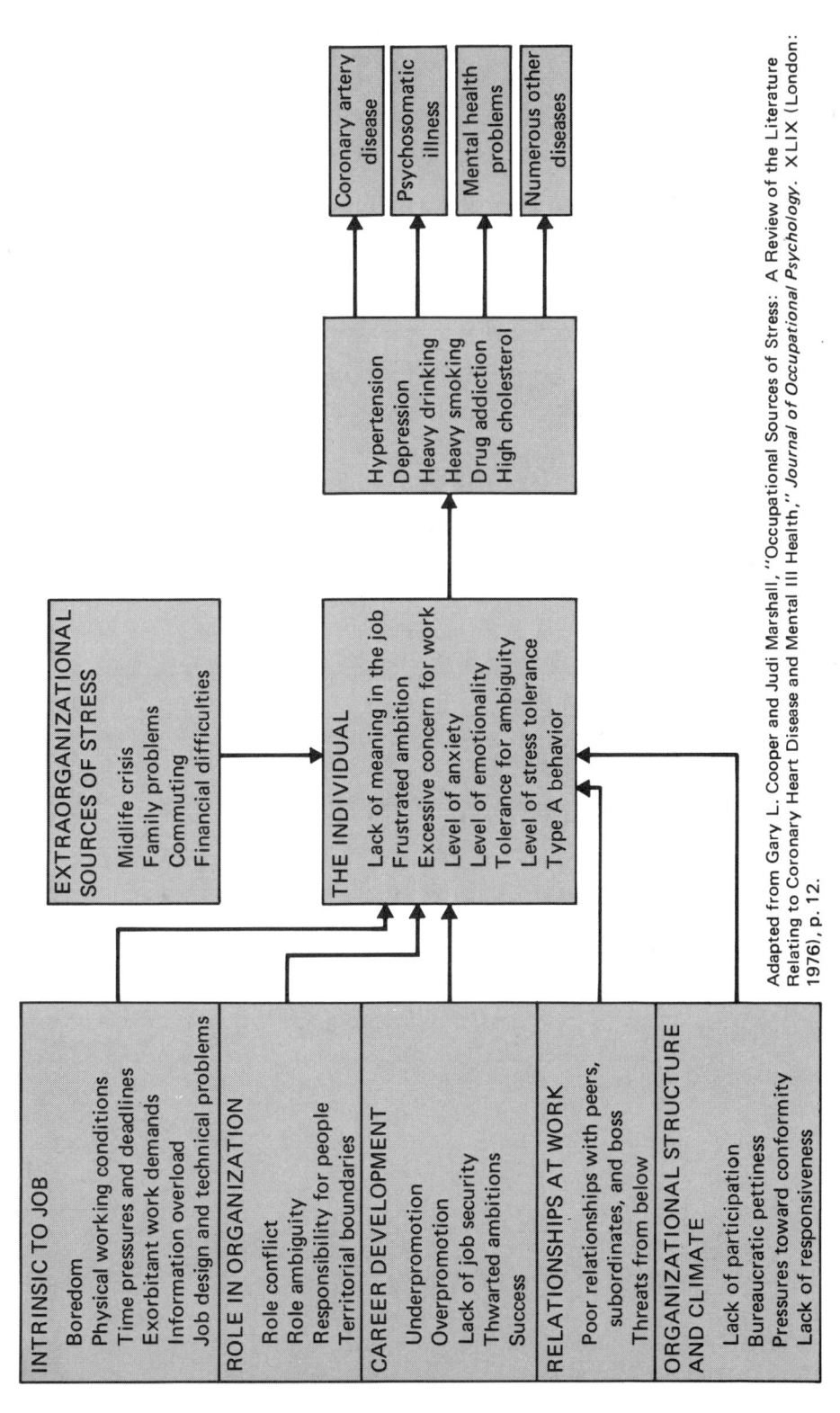

SOURCES OF STRESS AT WORK	PERSONAL STRESSORS	SYMPTOMS OF EXCESSIVE STRESS	DISEASE

INTRINSIC TO JOB
Boredom
Physical working conditions
Time pressures and deadlines
Exorbitant work demands
Information overload
Job design and technical problems

ROLE IN ORGANIZATION
Role conflict
Role ambiguity
Responsibility for people
Territorial boundaries

CAREER DEVELOPMENT
Underpromotion
Overpromotion
Lack of job security
Thwarted ambitions
Success

RELATIONSHIPS AT WORK
Poor relationships with peers, subordinates, and boss
Threats from below

ORGANIZATIONAL STRUCTURE AND CLIMATE
Lack of participation
Bureaucratic pettiness
Pressures toward conformity
Lack of responsiveness

EXTRAORGANIZATIONAL SOURCES OF STRESS
Midlife crisis
Family problems
Commuting
Financial difficulties

THE INDIVIDUAL
Lack of meaning in the job
Frustrated ambition
Excessive concern for work
Level of anxiety
Level of emotionality
Tolerance for ambiguity
Level of stress tolerance
Type A behavior

Hypertension
Depression
Heavy drinking
Heavy smoking
Drug addiction
High cholesterol

Coronary artery disease
Psychosomatic illness
Mental health problems
Numerous other diseases

Adapted from Gary L. Cooper and Judi Marshall, "Occupational Sources of Stress: A Review of the Literature Relating to Coronary Heart Disease and Mental Ill Health," *Journal of Occupational Psychology.* XLIX (London: 1976), p. 12.

image. Your career is the "critical mass" in realizing your potential.

■ *Exercise: Reviewing Your Mission*

Review the life mission statement you drafted in the last chapter. Is it still appropriate? If not, redraft it here.

_____
_____
_____
_____
_____
_____
_____
_____
_____
_____
_____
_____
_____
_____
_____
_____
_____
_____
_____
_____
_____
_____
_____
_____
_____
_____
_____

■

5. Positive Mental Attitude and Stress

Stress—what it is, how we perceive it, and how we handle it—is a fascinating but tricky subject. Let's see if we can pull it apart and understand how it operates in our lives.

Two people are running as fast as they can: the first is training for the 100-yard dash, the second is being chased by a mad dog.

Two people are executing a dance routine: the first is in a dance-exercise class, the second is auditioning for an important role in a musical comedy.

Two people are preparing the annual budget for their respective departments for the fifth year in a row: the first has had the same vice president to report to for five years, the second has a new one (the previous VP was fired).

It's obvious that the situation per se does not create the stress. It's the circumstances that surround it and the implications it holds for you personally.

If the runner being chased by a mad dog is confident of his running ability and has some reassurance that he is running toward a protected refuge, the stress will be moderate. But let's say that he has an irrational fear of mad dogs. Then, no matter how great a runner he is or how close the protection he is running toward, his stress will be as great as that of the poor runner.

When I talk about a positive response to stress, I don't mean that you should underestimate the dangers that exist for you in a given situation, and I'm not suggesting that you should evade your responsibilities or your less-than-spectacular ability to cope. Essentially it is a question of whether you meet the challenges of the day with courage and cheerfulness or with anxiety, discouragement, and frustration.

As that famous old fictional character David Harum put it: "A reasonable amount of fleas is good for a dog. Keeps him from brooding over being a dog." Stress in your life is like that. A reasonable amount is good for you—it keeps you in "fighting trim." But constant stress and unrelenting pressures are unreasonable in terms of your well-being because ultimately you are likely to start feeling angry and negative.

There is stress in everyone's life—if it's a meaningful life! In this chapter we'll try to understand the role stress plays and we'll try to find ways of reducing stress to a manageable level. But first let's identify some of the problems.

How Stress Affects Your Functioning

If a certain amount of stress is good for you and indeed even supplies energy, how can you tell how much is too much? Well, you can go by instinct for the most part. You know when things are getting out of hand. If you are called upon to make a speech, for example, and you know that appearing before a large group unnerves you, you can expect your mouth to go dry, your palms to sweat, your legs to feel weak. If this happens to you, you probably feel safest if you can read your entire presentation. It doesn't help at all to have people reassure you that you're great. The fact is that you have had a physical response that is beyond your intellectual control. Glucose has been released from your liver into your bloodstream and as a result your pulse rate, blood pressure, and respiration have had a sharp increase.

What can you do about it? If being unable to speak to an audience is a recurring problem to you, make up your mind to overcome it. People who want to get ahead must be able to appear before groups of other people. The more successful you are, the more likely it is that you will be invited to do so. Learn how.

First of all, be on very certain ground. Know your subject as well as possible—even better. If you depend on certain statistics to support your case, have them written on a card for easy reference. Don't stumble over things that you could easily avoid. If you don't know your subject to your complete comfort, allow yourself enough time to bone up. If you haven't got enough time, limit yourself ahead of time. Tell whoever extended the invitation that you will take on only one or two sections of the total discussion, the parts you really are an expert on.

If that doesn't calm you, try to analyze the cause of your anxiety. If you can't pin it down, try to speak to very small groups, perhaps six or eight people at first. Limit the audience to people you know. It's funny how much success succeeds, and if you have one or two good sessions with a small group, you will find it easy to expand little by little.

If nothing you do helps you overcome your stage fright, visit several professionals in speech making. They have a big bag of tricks and an excellent record of success.

The important thing in any set of circumstances is to pin down the cause of your stress. Analyze what has happened, and be completely honest with yourself. Don't attack others or place blame on them—it's your *reaction* you are trying to understand and change.

Stress and Your Health

It is well known that there is a direct relationship between emotions and physical health. It has been estimated that at least half of all illnesses are induced by emotions. A negative emotional response to pressure operating over a long period of time is far more dangerous than an illness that lasts a week or two.

The range of emotion-induced illnesses covers the spectrum of health care, including ulcers, high blood pressure, and heart disease.

A key element in stress is your mental attitude. React positively to pressure, nothing happens; react negatively, you get negative results. If you pass someone on the street who you believe has insulted you, a positive response would be to ignore him and not get charged up. But if you stop and seek a fight, you will increase your heart rate, raise your blood pressure, and change the chemistry of your body. According to Hans Selye:

> *Each period of stress, especially if it results from frustrating, unsuccessful struggles, leaves some irreversible chemical scars which accumulate to constitute the signs of tissue aging. But successful activity, no matter how intense, leaves virtually no such scars. On the contrary, it provides you with the exhilarating feeling of youthful strength, even at a very advanced age.**

Too much stress causes a power breakdown in your ability to function. Under severe stress, even the skilled professional performs poorly—the pianist's fingers jam up, the golf pro misses a two-foot putt, the high-powered executive has a heart attack, the salesman loses his "cool" and misses the sale. If stress is causing a power breakdown in your life, you should locate the source of the problem. The exercises and checkpoints in each chapter will help you trace the source of negative stress and provide some ideas for dealing with it.

> *God cures and the doctor takes the fee.*
> —Benjamin Franklin

Sir William Osler, one of the world's most eminent physicians, said, "No quality ranks with imperturbability. It means coolness and presence of mind under all circumstances. Imperturbability is a blessing to all. With practice and experience you may expect to attain a fair measure. The first essential is never to show or express anxiety or fear. Then these will probably pass."

*Selye, op. cit.

The message is very clear: If you hope to live a reasonably long and happy life, you must learn to respond positively to stress.

Stress and Sex

A healthy sex life is a natural way to ease stress and to release the tensions that build up as a result of modern life. If you don't have a satisfactory outlet for a healthy sex drive, you may well compound the problem of stress in your life. Some of the symptoms are irritability, an inability to concentrate, and increased tension.

If your sex life is good, it can improve your self-image, positive mental attitude, and sense of fulfillment. But if your sex life is poor or nonexistent, it can frustrate your efforts in other important areas of your life. Sex and love are highly subjective matters, and only you can decide whether they are relieving or inducing stress in your life and what, if anything, you should do about it.

A couple of generations ago the subject of sex was pushed under the rug. Discussion of it was almost nonexistent. Then came an ever-increasing outpouring of literature, films, and other material about sex, some of it wholesome and some offensive. But sexual freedom has shown, on the good side, that this innate and powerful urge is not only built into the human system but is also natural and extraordinarily fulfilling. While all other living creatures indulge in sex only when nature calls, only humans do so at any time for joy and fulfillment.

Should sex be a part of your strategic life planning? Yes, for several reasons. It takes two to tango, and when partners make sex a part of strategic planning, serious life problems can often be minimized or eliminated. When partners can discuss their differing needs and desires, when they begin to lose false modesty and inhibitions, and when they recognize that fulfilling sex is usually an imperative for a lasting relationship, the climb to the top of the mountain becomes more joyous.

Many years ago a friend called Bernard Baruch with this question: "Bernie, do you think there's as much love in the world today as there was years ago?"

"Yes," Baruch replied, "but there's another bunch doing it."

Type A or Type B?

Cardiologists Meyer Friedman and Ray H. Rosenman, in their book *Type A Behavior and Your Heart,* describe two general personality groupings: Type A and Type B. *Type A* personalities engage in a chronic struggle with time. They try to do the most in the shortest period of time. They are competitive and aggressive and usually have a "free-floating" form of hostility. They have tense facial muscles, are impatient and even explosive at times, and have a feeling of being under constant pressure. *Type B* personalities tend to be patient and unhurried. They work steadily, speak and move slowly. They are easygoing and not readily irritated.

Drs. Friedman and Rosenman present an impressive case that a Type A personality is two to three times more likely to suffer heart disease than a Type B personality. A Type A and a Type B may be under identical pressures, but the Type B will be meeting stress in a positive way without affecting his or her work or health.

By filling out the following questionnaire, you can get a good idea of whether you fall into the Type A or Type B class. If you are Type A—indicated by a preponderance of *yes* answers—it can literally be worth your life to change to a Type B.

■ Exercise: Assessing Your Personality Type

	Yes	No
1. Do you usually move, walk, and eat rapidly?	—	—
2. Do you often try to do two things at the same time?	—	—
3. Do you find it difficult to listen carefully?	—	—
4. Are you in general unaware of your surroundings?	—	—
5. Do you try to schedule more and more activities in less and less time?	—	—
6. Do you feel vaguely guilty when you are doing nothing?	—	—
7. Are you impatient, wanting things to happen faster than they do?	—	—
8. Are you easily riled?	—	—
9. Do you consciously feel under pressure most of the time?	—	—

Centuries ago Plutarch set forth his cure for some of the symptoms of Type A behavior. He said: "Let us cleanse the fountain of tranquility that is in ourselves. It does no good to rage at circumstances; events will take their course with no regard for us. Life is a game of chance in which we try, not only to throw what suits us best, but also, when we have thrown, to make good use of what turns up."

The Life Change Stress Test

There are many sources of stress outside your career. According to Drs. Thomas H. Holmes and Richard Rahe of the University of Washington School of Medicine, the rate of change in your life is related to the probability of change in your health. You can adjust to only so many life events in a period of time without encountering a high risk of illness or at least some change in your physical state.

Holmes and Rahe ranked 43 life events according to the degree of readjustment required. For example, being fired is twice as stressful as having trouble with the boss. The death of a spouse is twice as stressful as marriage. Although marriage is normally a pleasant source of stress, few events in life require as much adjustment as it does.

■ Exercise: Evaluating Life Changes

Record the appropriate score for life events you have experienced over the past year. Total your score.

Life Event	Mean Value	Your Score
1. Death of spouse	100	——
2. Divorce	73	——
3. Marital separation	65	——
4. Jail term	63	——
5. Death of close family member	63	——
6. Personal injury or illness	53	——
7. Marriage	50	——
8. Fired at work	47	——
9. Marital reconciliation	45	——
10. Retirement	45	——

Life Event	Mean Value	Your Score
11. Change in health of family member	44	___
12. Pregnancy	40	___
13. Sex difficulties	39	___
14. Gain of new family member	39	___
15. Business readjustment	39	___
16. Change in financial state	38	___
17. Death of close friend	37	___
18. Change to different line of work	36	___
19. Change in number of arguments with spouse	35	___
20. Mortgage over $30,000	31	___
21. Foreclosure of mortgage or loan	30	___
22. Change in responsibilities at work	29	___
23. Son or daughter leaving home	29	___
24. Trouble with in-laws	29	___
25. Outstanding personal achievement	28	___
26. Wife begin or stop work	26	___
27. Begin or end school	26	___
28. Change in living conditions	25	___
29. Revision of personal habits	24	___
30. Trouble with boss	23	___
31. Change in work hours or conditions	20	___
32. Change in residence	20	___
33. Change in schools	20	___
34. Change in recreation	19	___
35. Change in church activities	19	___
36. Change in social activities	18	___
37. Mortgage or loan less than $10,000	17	___
38. Change in sleeping habits	16	___
39. Change in number of family get-togethers	15	___
40. Change in eating habits	15	___
41. Vacation	13	___
42. Christmas	12	___
43. Minor violations of the law	11	___
Total		___

Adapted with permission from *Psychosomatic Research*, Volume 11, Thomas H. Holmes and R. H. Rahe, "The Social Readjustment Rating Score." Copyright © 1967, Pergamon Press, Ltd.

The authors of this chart have worked out the following table to show what the chances are that the specific stressful events will affect your physical health:

Fewer than 150 points	33 percent chance of a change in health
150–300 points	50 percent chance of a change in health
More than 300 points	80 to 90 percent chance of illness

That is a useful guideline, but some very important factors must be taken into consideration for a personal assessment. For example, no weight is given to your individual ability to cope with the events in your life. By far the most important factor in determining whether stress is good or bad for you is how *you* respond to it. In addition, the chart doesn't consider that problems tend to come in bunches. Getting a divorce certainly brings about other changes. Any or all of these could be brought into play: sex difficulties, change in financial status, trouble with in-laws, change in living conditions and personal habits, change in residence, changes in recreation and social activities, changes in sleeping and eating habits, and changes in the way you spend your vacation or celebrate Christmas. Imagine the impact if another major change, such as switching to a new job, occurred at the same time!

What can we learn from studying this chart and from examining our own lives in the light of what stress and change can mean? Certain changes we initiate; others are imposed on us by outside forces. But either way, change is inevitable in life.

The Holmes and Rahe study certainly suggests a high risk factor when too many changes occur too close together. So it's pretty obvious that you should keep certain important aspects of your life as stable as possible. Maintain as many anchor points as you can in the midst of an important change. Take advantage of the support old friends provide, and depend on old habits or comfortable activities for satisfaction.

Apply all the controls you can to minimize your stress.

Reducing Stress

It probably isn't very difficult for you to identify the stressful situations in your life—you know very well when you are feeling stress. What's more to the point is determining whether or not your stress is based on reality. That is, are you justified in feeling anxious and tense? After all, if a mad dog is chasing you, you would be foolish to think it's all in your head. What you must understand is whether the challenge is really beyond your ability or not, whether your antagonist is really so much better than you. Here we come back to goals and whether they are beyond our reach, and we come face to face with our self-image and the question of whether we have the self-confidence to meet the challenge head on.

The next exercise is designed to help you answer those questions. Select a situation that you know causes stress for you and try to examine as coolly as possible the objective and subjective factors that are relevant.

■ Exercise: Handling Stress

1. The situation that is causing particular stress in my life now is:

   _____
   _____
   _____
   _____

2. Is the resolution of the problem *really* very important to me, or am I exaggerating? (Analyze the realistic consequences, positive and negative.)

   _____
   _____
   _____
   _____

3. Would I be in a better position to succeed if I enlisted the help of someone else? If so, whom could I turn to?

   _____
   _____
   _____
   _____

4. Is there some way I can prepare myself for the next steps?

_____
_____
_____
_____
_____

5. If there is no way to reduce the strain, should I do my best to avoid having to face this situation again—or can I really handle it with just a little advance planning?

_____
_____
_____
_____
_____

■

We cannot eliminate real stress when it's based on reality, but we can keep ourselves from overreacting. When a difficult situation occurs, our emotions go into high gear as a way of arming us for the conflict. But by checking our emotions long enough to ask whether the situation is as threatening as we perceived it at first, we can exercise some control over the physiological responses of the nervous system.

In his classic, *Psycho-Cybernetics*, Maxwell Maltz discusses the problem of overresponse. He recommends that we practice the habit of not responding to negative emotions. He suggests that answering the telephone the minute it rings is an instinctive human response, and that we should learn to relax and not respond instantaneously. By letting the phone ring, you learn to delay your responses. Simply tell yourself to sit quietly and let it ring. "You create a built-in tranquilizer," Maltz says, "when you delay your response, when you just let your negative emotions 'ring off the hook'." Make the mental picture of not answering the phone your trigger to check overresponse.

Relaxation Techniques

In his famous Gifford lectures, William James cited example after example of people who had made a conscious effort to rid themselves of anxieties, worries, and feelings of inferiority and guilt. They found success only when they gave up the struggle and stopped trying to meet their problems head on.

> *The way to success, as vouched for by innumerable authentic personal narrations, is by surrender, passivity, not activity; relaxation, not intentness, should now be the rule. Give up the feelings of responsibility, let go your hold, resign the care of your destiny to higher powers, be genuinely indifferent as to what becomes of it all. . . . It is by giving your private convulsive self a rest and finding that a greater self is there. The results, slow or sudden, or great or small, of the combined optimism and expectancy, the regenerating phenomena which ensue on the abandonment of effort remain firm facts of human nature.**

Most people don't need to be persuaded that relaxation is important and beneficial, but they do need some help in learning how to achieve it. One of the best ways to achieve physical relaxation is through alternately tensing and relaxing a series of muscles. Here is how to do it.

Find a quiet place and get comfortable. Loosen restricting

---

*William James, *The Varieties of Religious Experience* (New York: Doubleday, 1978).

clothing, such as your belt and tie. Close your eyes and visualize a serene setting—a lake, a wide valley, horses grazing in a field. Now you will tense various muscles and hold the tension for 5 to 10 seconds. Before each exercise, breathe in, then tense and exhale slowly while you count seconds. At the end of the count, relax the muscles and feel the relaxation in those muscles quite consciously for 30 to 60 seconds. Think pleasant thoughts. You can be standing, sitting, or lying down when you begin the exercises.

1. Clench your fists and tense your arms.
2. Tilt your neck back and pull your shoulders toward your ears.
3. Clasp your hands in front of you at shoulder height and pull your shoulders down toward your waist.
4. Pull your stomach in tight, as if to touch your backbone.
5. Sitting down, extend your legs straight in front of you. Point your toes and tense your thighs.
6. Still sitting with your legs extended, bend your feet at the ankles until your toes are pointing back over your shoulders and tense your thighs.
7. Form an exaggerated grin and tighten your facial muscles.
8. Finally, combine all these exercises and tense all the major muscles at once. When you relax, sit quietly and consciously experience the flow of going slack all over. Remain motionless for a few minutes before you open your eyes and slowly move around.
9. Resume your normal routine.

If in the course of your day you become aware of tension, use this technique for quick, effective relaxation: Apply tension to hands and arms, legs and thighs, neck and shoulders and back, facial muscles and stomach muscles all at once. Hold 5 to 10 seconds as you expel air. Then relax. Do this a few times, then remain motionless in complete relaxation for as long as you like.

Mental Relaxation

If you are able to relax physically, you will find that a certain amount of mental relaxation comes naturally, but there are very good, effective techniques available to help. Here is one:

1. Close your eyes and relax your eyelids. Visualize the number 3 for a few seconds, then the number 2, finally the number 1. Breathe deeply.
2. Visualize a pleasant scene and concentrate on it with enjoyment.
3. Start counting down from 10 to 1, with your thumb touching your forefinger. Repeat the phrase with each number, either to yourself or aloud:

   10 I am very relaxed
    9 I am slowly sinking
    8 Deeper and deeper
    7 I am deeply relaxed
    6 I am slowly descending
    5 I feel very, very relaxed
    4 I am descending still deeper
    3 Very deeply now
    2 Deeper and deeper
    1 I am totally relaxed

Speak to yourself slowly, allowing the words and images to penetrate your mind. Let your words acquire meaning through anticipation of the results. After you have practiced this technique regularly for some time, you can become deeply relaxed by touching your thumb and forefinger and saying the word *relax*. You may find it helpful to tape-record these two exercises and play them at night before you go to sleep. You must repeat the exercises regularly if they are to become a habit.

Another excellent relaxation technique is Transcendental Meditation, commonly known as TM. The goal of TM is to quiet

---

Why not a relaxation break instead of a coffee break? Even a short break is beneficial, whether it's used for exercise, muscle tension and release, or mental relaxation. Whatever method you use, you will find yourself refreshed and better able to cope with the job at hand.

As you go through the day, observe yourself at frequent intervals. Try to catch yourself when you are wasting energy through nervous habits and tensed muscles. Stop in your tracks and calmly order all tense muscles to relax. And don't be afraid to repeat the order.

the body and clear the mind by concentrating on a specific word or sound. It's like turning the television set off. You mentally "tune out" your normal mental pictures for 15 minutes. Meditation can put you in touch with yourself, and many people have found it both pleasurable and beneficial. If you are seriously interested in practicing TM, seek out one of the many books already published on the subject.

You can achieve very similar results by using the much simpler technique developed by Herbert Benson in his book *The Relaxation Response*. Choose a time of day or evening when you can be sure you won't be interrupted in any way for 5 to 15 minutes. Then:

1. Get comfortable and close your eyes.
2. Relax deeply. Touch your thumb and forefinger and count down from 10 to 0.
3. Breathe normally and become aware of your breathing.
4. Each time you exhale, say the word *one* to yourself.
5. Continue for a comfortable period of time, keeping your eyes closed and feeling totally free of physical tension.

Dr. Chandra Patel of the University of London's School of Hygiene reported that in a study of 192 British workers, training in breathing exercises, deep muscle relaxation, and mental relaxation in the form of meditation significantly lowered blood pressure and reduced the incidence of heart attacks. Dr. Patel said, "It also helps people handle their day-to-day stress by integrating relaxation into everyday life."

In his book *Stress Without Distress*, Hans Selye offers these stress-reduction techniques:

1. Concentrate on the pleasant side of life.
2. Fight for only those things that are really worth the effort.
3. Don't try to be a perfectionist.
4. When you fail, reestablish your self-confidence by remembering past accomplishments.
5. Don't procrastinate. Get the unpleasant things out of the way.
6. Value the simple things of life.
7. Don't waste time trying to befriend those who don't want your love and friendship.
8. Earn your neighbor's love.

Tension Relievers

Exercise. Walking, riding a bicycle, deep breathing, and calisthenics are very beneficial in reducing tension if they are done regularly. Such activities revitalize and refresh you.

Learn to laugh at yourself. Bob Hope has said that one of the reasons he is a happy man is that he doesn't take himself too seriously. You can free yourself of tension by developing the ability to laugh, silently or aloud, in moments of stress.

Take up a sport or hobby. Golf, tennis, baseball, and other sports provide release from pressure. Activities such as singing and dancing, working with the hands, talking, and writing can also be helpful.

> When down in the mouth remember Jonah. He came out all right.
> —Thomas Edison

Indulge yourself. At times a certain amount of self-pampering can be good for you. An occasional splurge on something unusual can make you feel better. In most cases, however, it's best to face the problem directly and resolve it.

Stress and Life Planning

Later in this book we will be talking a great deal about strategic life planning, something that is essential in dealing with stress. By coordinating your life strategies, you will be attacking the problem of stress automatically, because you will:

1. Eliminate gnawing confusion over which course to take and when.
2. Develop an overall life plan that will place things in perspective for you.
3. Set priorities for all your goals.
4. Develop strategies to meet your problems and goals.
5. Develop the skills you'll need to achieve your goals.

> Laughter is one of the best ways of improving health and relieving stress. A study at Northwestern University showed that the act of laughing helps breathing, stimulates circulation, and massages the heart. Laughter also improves digestion, aids blood pressure problems, and prolongs life. The old adage is still true: "Laugh and the world laughs with you. Cry and you cry alone." When we apply humor to our personal problems and to the tensions of our lives, we help both ourselves and others. Humor turns off tension and is extremely effective in countering stress.

People talk about and admire those who "have it all together." Medical cases abound of patients who survive severe diseases because they have a reason for living. Those without goals often don't pull through. History is replete with examples of men and women who were able to overcome great obstacles because they had a goal. Prisoners of war survive torture and inhuman conditions because they have a will to live, a reason for being.

If you seriously undertake all the exercises in this book, you will arrive at a positive stress-coordinated life plan that can bring you peace of mind, satisfaction, and personal fulfillment.

Personal Stress Control Record

It will be well worth your time to track your personal stress pattern for a week or two. Set aside a few minutes each night before retiring to think about and record your stressful experiences of the day. At the same time, try to improve your relaxation techniques. After a week or so, evaluate your responses to stress and trace the effect of negative stress on your other activities.

> By coordinating and integrating your "assets," you can provide a stable foundation for the management of stress in your life. By clarifying who you are and where you are going and then creating an action program, you begin to harmonize your life's activities and encourage a natural flow of inner peace and energy.

Stress Control Record

Check your stress level each day.

Day	Great 10 9 8	Relaxed 7 6 5	Tense 4 3 2	Disaster 1 0	What happened today to affect your score?
1					
2					
3					
4					
5					
6					
7					

Check the results of your relaxation exercises.

Day	Great 10 9 8	Relaxed 7 6 5	Tense 4 3 2	Disaster 1 0	Notes on your feelings during or after exercise
1					
2					
3					
4					
5					
6					
7					

■ Exercise: Managing Stress

After evaluating your responses to stress and to problems, think about what you might do to manage stress more effectively. List a few ideas here and begin putting them to work for you.

1. _____
   _____
2. _____
   _____
3. _____
   _____
4. _____
   _____
5. _____
   _____

■

Review:
Your Positive Mental Attitude

Now that you've completed this section on the first checkpoint of potential, quickly score yourself by answering the following questions, using the scale at the bottom of the page.

1. Do you have a strong desire to realize potential? ___
2. Can you define your central life purpose? ___
3. Are you suited to this purpose? ___
4. Is pursuing this purpose enjoyable to you? ___
5. Are you skillful at pursuing your purpose? ___
6. Are you a positive person? ___
7. Do you believe in yourself? ___
8. Do you like your career? ___
9. Is your career your primary successful activity? ___
10. Are you undecided about your career? ___
11. Do you respond positively to stress? ___
12. Do you use relaxation to your advantage? ___
13. Do you use tension to your advantage? ___

Scale

	10	Full use of potential
YES	9	Almost there
	8	Above average
	7	Average
	6	Below average
	5	
NO	4	
	3	Help!
	2	
	1	
	0	

Answer these questions about your responses to the questions above:

    Score 8–10   Am I satisfied?
                                Do I still want to improve?
                                How can I improve?
    Score 6–7   Is this acceptable to me?
                                Is it important to improve?
                                How can I improve?
    Score 5 or below   What's happening? Why?
                                Is it important to improve?
                                How can I improve?

If you've identified any areas for improvement, answer the questions below:

    With whom can I discuss this problem?
    Who can give me counsel or direction in solving the problem?
    What step can I take *now* to do something to solve the problem?

Review Notes

Quickly review the marginal notes you have made and the exercises and activities you have done in this section. Summarize your thoughts below:

1. Ideas for follow-up developed as you read this section:

    _____
    _____
    _____
    _____

2. Ideas you believe should be included in your coordinated action plan:

    _____
    _____
    _____
    _____

3. Thoughts that occur to you at this time about

    (a) Your positive mental attitude:

    (b) Having a strong purpose in your life:

    (c) Your belief and confidence in yourself:

    (d) Your career:

    (e) Stress in your life:

(f) Your ability to use mental and physical relaxation in a positive way:

_____
_____
_____
_____

_____

4. Other thoughts:

_____
_____
_____
_____
_____

Additional Reading

One action step available to help you improve is to learn more about an area suggested in this section. Here is a list of books you might consider for additional study:

The Magic of Believing by Claude M. Bristol. New York: Cornerstone Library, 1971
The Power of Positive Thinking by Norman Vincent Peale. New York: Fawcett World Library, 1956
Stress Without Distress by Hans Selye. Philadelphia: J.B. Lippincott, 1974.
Managing Stress by Jere E. Yates. New York: AMACOM, 1979.
Career Satisfaction and Success by Bernard Haldane. New York: AMACOM, 1974.
The Relaxation Response by Herbert Benson. New York: William Morrow & Company, 1975.
Type A Behavior and Your Heart by Meyer F. Friedman and Ray H. Rosenman. New York: Alfred A. Knopf, 1974.
Self Renewal by John W. Gardner. New York: Harper & Row, 1964.
See You at the Top by Zig Ziglar. Gretna, La., 1979.

SECTION III

Checkpoint 2: Your Goals

I have found that helping people to develop personal goals has proved to be the most effective way to help them to cope with problems.

—Ari Kiev, MD

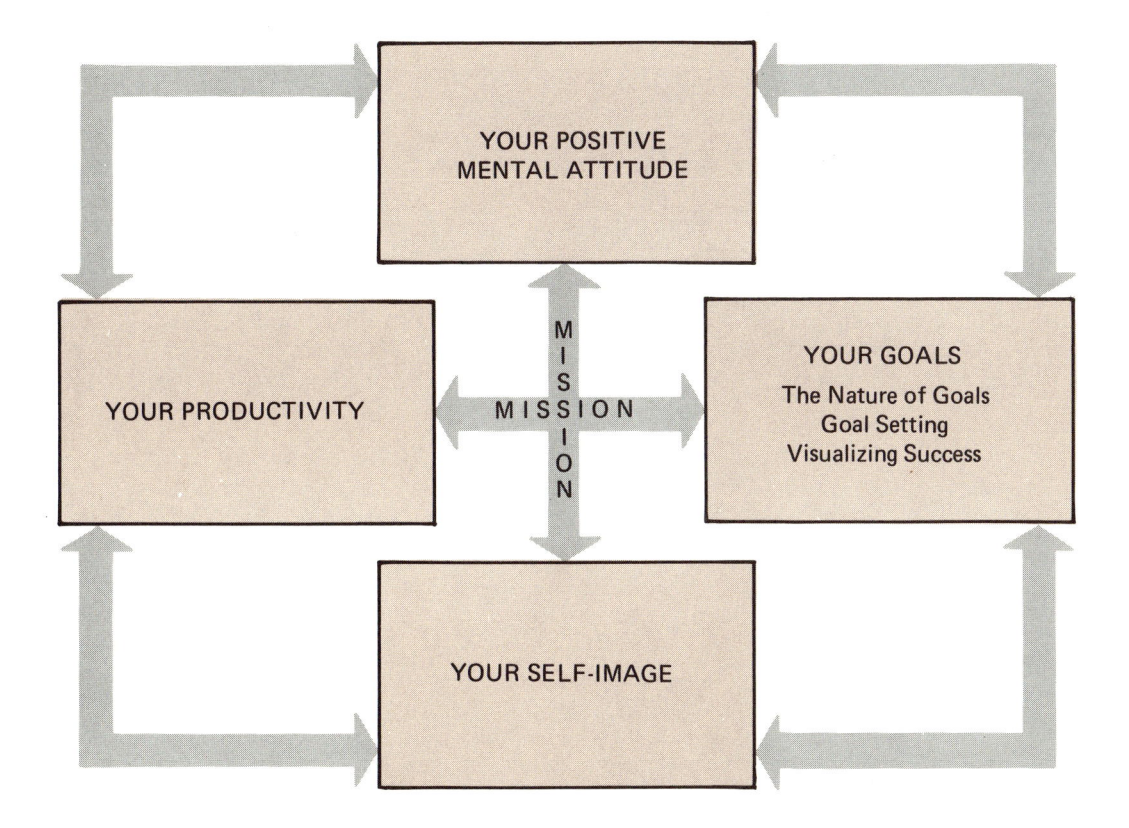

```
                    ┌─────────────────────┐
                    │   YOUR POSITIVE     │
                    │   MENTAL ATTITUDE   │
                    └─────────────────────┘
                              ↕
                              M
                              I
┌──────────────────┐          S          ┌──────────────────────┐
│                  │          S          │    YOUR GOALS        │
│ YOUR             │ ← MISSION →         │  The Nature of Goals │
│ PRODUCTIVITY     │          I          │    Goal Setting      │
│                  │          O          │  Visualizing Success │
└──────────────────┘          N          └──────────────────────┘
                              ↕
                    ┌─────────────────────┐
                    │   YOUR SELF-IMAGE   │
                    └─────────────────────┘
```

6. The Nature of Goals

There is no achievement without goals. Perhaps through some magical piece of luck or coincidence you will manage a great coup someday, but coincidence is not something you'll want to put your money on. It's safe to say that without knowing where you want to go, and without making some specific plans about how to get there, you will either move backward or drift sideways.

Goals provide the game plan for effectively coordinating and using your time and your energy, and goals root your commitment. Goals energize the human system and generate persistent, progressive activity. Just as soon as a concrete goal is set and some concrete plans are made, no matter how short range, activity begins. When you set goals for yourself, you take charge of your life.

In his book *See You at the Top,* Zig Ziglar points out that while it is safer not to set goals and therefore not to be embarrassed in front of friends or associates, it would also be safer for a ship to stay in port or a plane to stay on the ground. But the ship would collect barnacles and become unseaworthy faster in the harbor, and the plane would deteriorate and rust much faster on the ground.

Setting Realistic and Challenging Goals

Goals should enable you to grow, but without excessive stress. They should therefore be based on a true assessment of your personal development, abilities, and circumstances at a given time. The goal "I want to earn $35,000 by the end of next year" may or may not be realistic. If you are currently making $15,000 a year, it is probably unrealistic to expect to jump to $35,000. But if you are earning $25,000 a year now, a $10,000 jump may well be within reach.

> Have you noticed how comfortable it is to work within your present performance limits? The term "comfort zone" aptly describes these limits. Setting a goal beyond a comfort level of performance takes courage and effort. How much easier it is to stay at a lower level, to be comfortable, to avoid the risks and failures that go with challenge and growth.

By experiencing small successes with realistic, clearly defined goals, you gradually move up to more difficult goals. There is great truth to the saying "Nothing succeeds like success." As you string together small successes, you create a "winning mentality" that carries over to other aspects of your life.

What is a challenging goal? It is one that makes you grow. Many experts agree you should have a fifty-fifty chance of achieving a particular goal—which is to say that a goal should be on the high side but still within reason. One of the most common stumbling blocks to goal setting is fear of failure.

> *Every now and then a man's mind is stretched by a new idea and never shrinks back to its former dimensions.*
> —Oliver Wendell Holmes

Goals and Purpose

Realizing your potential is a goal you'll never completely achieve. It is a direction you take in life, not a destination. Human potential is great, and you can hardly begin to explore it in a lifetime.

The ability to live fully and renew yourself is best attained by having a purpose in life—a sense of mission larger than your

---

Tips from the Pros

Art Linkletter, in his book *Yes, You Can*, describes four principles he has found helpful in arriving at his life goals:

1. Success is a journey, not a destination.
2. Make your goals specific but don't set them in concrete. Be prepared for the unexpected.
3. True success always results in some measure of happiness.
4. Reaching a goal should always make you a better person.

Warren Spahn, the Hall of Fame pitcher who set many records, offers this formula for setting and achieving goals:

1. Don't baby yourself! Give it everything and keep trying for success.
2. Have a goal of excellence—20 wins a year, for example. You never get far going for average.
3. Cultivate the ability to break through the fatigue barrier. Push through to a new surge of energy.
4. Pay the price for what you want. Have the discipline and physical determination.

immediate interests and needs. When you commit yourself fully to discovering your potential, you begin to grow, to become something larger than yourself. This is sometimes observed in people who feel they have a "calling" and who have a talent for living the full life. The most meaningful goals are attained when people regard their own lives as meaningful.

Herbert A. Otto, in his book *Guide to Developing Your Potential*, says, "There is every reason to conclude that lack of purpose in life and the absence of clearly formulated goals which transcend the narrow scope of the individual are deeply inimical to the development of potential."* Exploring your potential adds new dimensions to your life and can be downright enjoyable, even exciting. You haven't the time to be bored, because it's like drilling and finding an inexhaustible source of energy.

■ Exercise: Focusing Your Goals

1. Write a statement describing what you would like to do with your life. In it, come to grips with your own mortality. You will find your vision exploding from the narrowness of "now" to include the whole fabric of your being. It can provide an entirely new perspective on your life.

_____
_____
_____
_____
_____
_____
_____
_____
_____
_____
_____
_____

*Hollywood, Calif.: Wilshire Book Co., 1973.

2. Write a statement describing what you have done in your career up to this point. Describe your skills, your activities, and your achievements. Talk about what you are proud of. Discuss what else you hope to achieve. Write your thoughts down informally, boast about yourself, and have fun.

_____
_____
_____
_____
_____
_____
_____
_____
_____
_____
_____

3. Write a statement describing what you have done with your life *outside* your career. Describe your hobbies, social relationships, and recreational and educational pursuits. If you feel you need to broaden your outside interests, list several new areas you would like to pursue. What steps can you take to expand your cultural, intellectual, and social horizons?

_____
_____
_____
_____
_____
_____
_____
_____
_____
_____
_____

■

Goals and Determination

A young reporter once asked Thomas Edison how it felt to have failed ten thousand times with a new invention. Edison said, "Young man, since you are just starting out in life, I will tell you something of benefit. I have not failed ten thousand times. I have successfully found ten thousand ways that will not work." Edison estimated that he performed more than fourteen thousand experiments in perfecting the incandescent lamp.

> *Always think of what you have to do as easy and it will become so.*
> —Emile Coué

What can we learn from that? If Edison's long-range goal was to discover how to make the incandescent bulb, think what singlemindedness, what determination, what unswerving dedication he possessed. He had in mind a certain end result, but clearly he had to solve many problems before he could even approach the final product. He spent years working away at it, approaching it from every conceivable angle, until he solved each of the problems he met along the way. He had many short-range goals that had to be reached before he could approach the big, final goal that was indeed a crowning achievement—one that changed the way people lived.

To minimize your chances of failing with a difficult goal, you need dogged determination. Dwell on your goal; become enthusiastic about it. Use the techniques in this book to develop an action plan that excites you. As you read, remember that you are trying to discover more about yourself and the subtle interplay between your goals, skills, and strengths.

The process of discovery depends on many small things: Alexander Graham Bell is credited as having invented the telephone, but a man named Phillip Reis also came close to success. The little difference was the turn of a screw. Reis didn't know that if he had turned a single screw one quarter of a turn, he would have transformed interrupted current into continuous current. Then he would have been known as the inventor of the telephone.

Have the courage to make that last turn of the screw that locks in your goal. When you seek your goals with a positive mental attitude, you keep trying. You keep searching for something more. The failure gives up too soon, often right on the edge of a breakthrough.

Goals and Self-Belief

Why do those who succeed seem to have the magic touch? Why do many talented people fail in life, while others, less talented, achieve so much? One answer: desire and self-belief.

The critical forces in the pursuit of any goal are your belief in yourself and your desire to achieve. What you believe yourself to be, you are. The way you walk, dress, and talk shows how you think. For example, if you are ill and you feel certain that you'll recover, the odds are in your favor.

Many people start out with a clearly defined, realistic goal, but they fail to sustain it. It is extremely difficult to hold on to a mental picture of success for a long period of time. Because of this and in spite of their best intentions, people often do not follow through with a goal once the novelty wears off. You must utilize the power of "sustained belief" in achieving your goals.

Abraham Lincoln, during the dark days of the Civil War, told

Do You Believe?

A young man fell from a ledge while mountain climbing. As he fell, he saved his life by grabbing a sturdy limb and hanging on. He looked up and said:
"Lord, help me!"
A voice boomed through the ravine: "Do you believe?"
The young man said, "I believe."
The voice boomed: "Do you *really* believe?"
"Yes, I really believe," he replied.
"Then let go of the limb," the voice boomed.
After a moment's pause, the young man looked up and said, "Is there anybody else up there who can help me?"

> *Qualities of Success*
>
> A study conducted by Dr. Albert Shapiro of the University of Texas Graduate School of Business identified five traits common to successful businesspeople:
>
> - Self-motivated doers set long-range goals but don't dwell on them. Most of the time they concentrate on day-to-day implementation.
> - They don't worry. The possibility of failure is taken for granted; it's nothing to worry about.
> - They don't intimidate themselves by setting grandiose goals and overwhelming challenges.
> - They don't set limited working hours.
> - Outwardly, they tend to be modest and chalk off their achievements to "luck," but inwardly they have a strong belief in their power over events.
>
> *Executive Digest,* May 5, 1980

this story: "Years ago a young friend and I were out one night when a shower of meteors fell from a clear November sky. The young man was concerned, but I told him to look up in the sky past the shooting stars to the fixed stars beyond, shining serene in the firmament, and I said, 'Let us not mind the meteors, but let us keep our eyes on the stars.'"

Goals and Money

The principles of successful activity apply equally to those who are paid money and those who are not (the housewife, retiree, or student). However, money is a powerful factor in developing inner resources and in reaching goals.

Profits or monetary incentives help spark one of our most powerful drives—the desire to excel and to achieve. In addition to providing us with the necessities as well as the finer things in life, money is an instant yardstick of how well we are doing. It is also a primary basis for distributing respect in our society. While we may at times decry the "bottom line" concept in business, with its emphasis on net profits, it is still a sound approach to developing human resources for the benefit of all.

If you can't realize your potential in the United States, where else are you likely to do so?

It is always important to have some measure of progress toward a goal. In addition to money and other numerical measures (such as the stopwatch for the swimmer or the scorecard for the golfer), progress can be measured in terms of actions or behavior—for example, getting along better with your associates or being more tolerant with family members. There is also the more subtle measure of personal satisfaction. A goal can be extraordinarily important simply because it is personally rewarding.

7. Goal Setting

All of us are subject to the shock of rapid change. Today we are increasingly bombarded by events beyond our control. Inflation, recession, and other outside stresses impinge on our emotions. When we add these events to career, family, health, financial, and personal problems it is apparent why stress "overload" is such a common problem. But while future shock is here, with its rapid changes, the delicate human nervous system remains unchanged. People are continually searching for firm ground on which to stand and meet these problems.

The truth is that if you don't have a goal-oriented game plan for your life you may well lose control of those events over which you can exercise control. For example, you may feel reasonably secure in your career today. But are you prepared for a second or perhaps a third career if circumstances make such a decision necessary? Sure, things are OK now: "I don't have to worry about my job" or "I have a happy married life." But things happen unexpectedly—career crises, health problems, family problems—and without planning you end up being a reactor rather than an actor in life.

Bernie Parent, one of the greatest goalies in National Hockey League history, recently told the story of his forced retirement from the Philadelphia Flyers in February 1979, after a crippling eye injury. He described how his world was shattered and how he began looking for happiness at the bottom of a bottle. Today Parent, 35, is on the road back. He has joined Alcoholics Anonymous and hasn't had a drink for months. He says, "There is a built-in discipline to playing any sport, a structure that keeps you within bounds. All of a sudden I couldn't play any more. The discipline was gone and it was easy to drift away. . . . Suddenly I was no longer Bernie Parent, the hockey player. I wasn't prepared to be Bernie Parent, the human being. I wasn't prepared to deal with reality."

His association with AA has taught him to face reality. "I'm not going on who I used to be," Parent says. "Now I'm interested in who I'm going to be." Parent is earnestly pursuing a career in public relations with the Flyers. He is taking public speaking courses and an English course with Berlitz to improve his delivery. Right now Bernie is picking up the pieces of his life. It may be the biggest save he ever made.

> *Perfection of means and confusion of goals seem—in my opinion—to characterize our age.*
> —Albert Einstein

The Purpose of Setting Goals

Comprehensive goal setting accomplishes several important objectives:

1. It makes you an active agent in molding your life. The pleasure of taking control of your life is, by itself, worth the effort.
2. It enables you to be clear on what you want. Not much in life is accomplished without specific goals.
3. It prepares you for the inevitable changes that occur as you pass from decade to decade—marriage, children, career changes, retirement, and so on.
4. It gives you a full perspective on your life. You can see (perhaps for the first time) whether or not you are structuring your life to realize your potential and achieve personal fulfillment.

> *When you have a choice to make and don't make it, that in itself is a choice.*
> —William James

As you complete the various exercises in this book, you will be pinpointing your goals in an organized way rather than in haphazard fashion. Keep in mind that the process is always flexible and should be enjoyable. You need room to be spontaneous, to be able to meet the unexpected, to be able to roll with the punches, and to be ready for the random event. You need time to smell the flowers and to enjoy the scenery as you climb your mountain.

As you develop your goals, remember that you're not just doing it for yourself. Your family, your associates, your friends will be affected. You're going to be happier and you'll bring more happiness to others.

Principles of Goal Setting

While goal setting can be a sophisticated and highly personal process, certain principles common to both business and personal goals are fundamental to successful goal achievement. Here are some key principles for setting winning goals:

Define Your Goals Clearly. The failure to establish clear goals is one of the chief obstacles to achievement and personal fulfillment. Make your goals positive and specific. ("I *will* plan my day so I have more time for leisure." "I *will* improve my productivity by 10 percent this year.") Throughout this book you will be evaluating your strengths and weaknesses, your career goals, your aims for your family, your social and interpersonal relationships, and your leisure activities. The objective (and it is so important) is to enable you to clarify your goals and set priorities.

The art of goal setting lies in your ability to focus on one well-defined objective at a time. It is like using a magnifying glass to focus the sun's rays on a single spot so you can start a fire. Move the magnifying glass constantly and it loses its power. Much of what you accomplish in life will depend on your ability to concentrate on a specific target until you achieve your objective.

At a meeting some years ago, a speaker asked members of the audience to hold their breath as long as they could, and he timed them. Afterward, he said to the group, "Now look at your watches and hold your breath for three minutes." With a clear objective in mind, the members of the audience held their breath far longer than they did on the first try. The point is, of course, that the more clearly you define your target, the easier it is to concentrate on and achieve it.

A clearly defined goal is one that is specific and measurable and one that is set within a specific time frame. The following statement illustrates a poorly defined goal: "I want to earn a good living." What does the term "good living" mean? How much income do you need, and in what period of time? How will your expenses relate to the income you want to earn? By what time do you wish to earn this so-called good living?

Contrast this with the statement "I want to be earning $35,000 a year by the end of next year." This goal is definite and sets a time limit for achievement. In other words, there is a specific target to shoot for and a specific period of time in which to hit it.

Put Your Goals in Writing. Clearly defined, *written* goals are the tools for achievement and fulfillment. These goals must mesh with your commitment and your purpose in life. Losers don't set goals, don't define them, and don't put them in writing.

> Maximize your life by setting goals. This is no magic formula; it's just plain common sense. When you blend your skills, your achievements, and your goals, you bring a perspective to your life that otherwise might not be possible.

Successful people in all walks of life have found that writing down their goals can provide the energy and the will to achieve them. Writing down goals forces you to be specific. Your goals become more real and you avoid the dangers of vague, indefinite objectives.

Henry J. Kaiser, in a commencement address at the University of Nevada, gave as his number-one recommendation: "Know yourself and decide what you most of all want to make out of your life. Then *write down* your goals and plan to reach them." Wallace Johnson, founder of the Holiday Inn chain, attributed his success to prayer, hard work, talking to himself about his goals, and "making a list of things I want to do."

Record Baseline Data. In setting goals, you need specific information about your present actions in order to establish a basis for change. For example, if your goal is to double the amount of time you spend walking each week, keep track of the time you currently spend walking and figure the average. Thus:

Day	Minutes Spent Walking
1	19
2	15
3	12
4	20
5	25
6	18
7	15
Total	124
Average	18 min. per day

In the business or professional world, baseline data are kept as a matter of course. The salesman knows how many calls he makes a week, the doctor how many patients he sees. But few of us keep such data on our personal lives. It is important to have a complete and accurate record of where you stand now if you are to establish a goal for change.

In setting baseline data, keep these points in mind:

1. Don't rely on memory. Make a record as it occurs.
2. Give yourself a long enough period of time to get a fair average.
3. Be specific. Vague entries are useless.

> In *Alice in Wonderland,* Alice asks the Cheshire Cat for directions:
> "Would you tell me, please, which way I ought to go from here?"
> "That depends a good deal on where you want to get to," says the cat.
> "I don't much care where," says Alice.
> "Then it doesn't matter which way you go," says the cat.

4. Note all the circumstances when you are gathering data—the time of day, who was there, where it occurred, and other pertinent information.

Good baseline information is the foundation for setting successful goals.

Break Goals into Subgoals. Trying to make the transition from present performance to a desired goal in a single jump can lead to early failure and loss of confidence. Subgoals are the steppingstones to success. For example, if your goal is to double the amount of time you spend walking per day, you might set a graduated plan like this for one week:

Day	Minutes Spent Walking
1	18—Baseline
2	21
3	24
4	27
5	30
6	33
7	36—Goal

The following exercise will help you bring your plans and dreams into sharper focus. Remember, the job of constructing a life plan is yours. Only you can design a lifetime strategy and an action program to answer the questions below. Your program

> *All my successes have been built on my failures.*
> —Benjamin Disraeli

will change as you grow, as you journey through each decade of life and confront your own special problems and opportunities.

Reinforcing Goal Setting

A "big goal" is not a measure of your present status. It is a target, something you mean to attain ultimately. You don't feel like a failure if the goal is not achieved tomorrow or the next day.

You also need smaller, short-range goals which are just beyond your current ability but still within the realm of "present possibility." These goals can be very supportive and satisfying as they help you build your "winning streak." Most important, they provide a foundation for successful activity. Here are some examples of specific short-range goals:

"I will increase production by 10 percent by the end of a month."
"I will call on 6 prospects each day for 30 days."
"I will swim half an hour each day for the next 30 days."

When you successfully complete each task, immediately reinforce your commitment by giving yourself a little "reward." Make it a selfish reward. Buy yourself a new putter. Take your spouse to a fancy restaurant. Go to a ballgame. Telephone a

---

A Scientist's Approach to Setting Goals

Dr. Leonard Ross, chairman of the anatomy department of the Medical College of Pennsylvania, heads a scientific team armed with a multimillion-dollar grant to study the human brain. Talking about his research in a recent interview, Ross says, "Breakthroughs in our research are neither startling nor recognized when they take place. Usually you don't know until later, maybe years later."

How does a scientist come to grips with such long-range problems? Ross explains, "What I try to do is to take a big field and break it up into many small questions. Then I might say to myself, 'What small question am I going to ask today?' That's the way we get our satisfaction. We stick the big questions at the back of our heads and look at the little questions."

friend. Do something special you feel good about. (Let your spouse share your good feeling—you need all the support you can get.)

These small reinforcements provide momentum and keep you on track. As most good actors will tell you, applause from the audience ("reinforcement") does much more than make them *want* to perform better—it actually *helps* them to do so. Under proper stimulation from an audience, a fine actor can surpass himself.

The science of psychology has demonstrated the value of reinforcement. Research has shown that if a desired action is immediately followed by a positive reward, it is more likely to be repeated. It is the speed rather than the size of the reward that is important.

This principle has long been used in the business world in increased salary, deferred compensation, stock plans, and various other perquisites. Be your own boss and use reinforcement to help you reach your goals. The big rewards will follow.

8. Visualizing Success

The Nature of Visualization

An important step in building self-confidence is being able to see yourself as a success. When you are goal-oriented, you tend to move in the direction of your mindset. If you think you are a failure, you probably will be. If you think you are a success, you very well may be. Certainly, your chances are better.

Developing a positive image of yourself is vital to success. If you play a sport, you know that lack of self-confidence can kill your game. Knute Rockne once said that most people thought there had to be either good losers or bad winners. "Show me a good loser," he said, "and I'll show you a loser. Give me eleven lousy losers and I'll give you a national championship football team."

> A Major Naismith, prisoner of war in North Vietnam, spent several years in solitary confinement. After a few months, he realized he would have to occupy his mind if he was to retain his sanity. A 90s golfer, he mentally selected his favorite golf course and each day, for four hours, played a full 18 holes. He visualized his clothing, the weather conditions, his golfing companions. He saw the turf, the trees, the birds.
>
> He visualized each shot he made. He kept his left arm straight, his head steady, his takeaway slow. He "saw" a smooth downswing, kept his eye on the ball, and visualized the flight of the ball down the fairway to the exact spot he had aimed for.
>
> Every step of each round was meaningful to him. He did this seven days a week for over five years. When he was finally released and played his first game of golf, he shot an amazing 74!

A major factor in developing faith in yourself is to literally saturate your mind with positive thoughts. Visualize your goal and the steps necessary to achieve it. Remember, it's not necessarily what you see; it's what you believe you see. Once you form the image of a goal, your mind acts on that mental picture automatically.

In essence, visualization is a total thought process that puts meaning into your goals by pointing you in the direction you want to go. Whether your goal is to improve your golf swing, to make more money, or to be more productive, your ability to imagine, to dream—to visualize what success will be like—will accelerate your progress.

Some of our greatest scientific discoveries arose from the willingness to dream. Michael Faraday, one of the founders of electromagnetic theory, used to picture himself as an atom under pressure and gained insight into the electrolyte. Einstein daydreamed about what would happen if man could fly into space at the speed of light. From this image he developed some important features of his theory of relativity. Engineer Charles Kettering, trying to determine why kerosene "knocked" more than gasoline, had a visual image of a flower, the trailing arbutus, which blooms early in spring even beneath the snow. Its red coloration, which absorbs heat faster than other hues, gave him the idea for tetraethyl lead.

Steps in the Visualization Process

The key to visualizing a goal is to create positive mental images while the mind is in its most receptive state. How do we know when that is? Science tells us. Brain waves can be measured by an electroencephalograph in cycles per seconds (cps). They break down into four basic types:

$$\begin{aligned}
14 \text{ or more cps} &= \text{beta waves} \\
7\text{--}13 \text{ cps} &= \text{alpha waves} \\
4\text{--}7 \text{ cps} &= \text{theta waves} \\
\text{Below } 4 \text{ cps} &= \text{delta waves}
\end{aligned}$$

"Beta" waves occur when you are wide awake; "delta" waves occur during deep sleep. Your best bet is to totally relax in the "alpha" state, and occasionally the "theta" state, while you are awake. It is in this relaxed condition that you are most creative and can visualize most effectively.

1. Use the relaxation procedure outlined in Chapter 5 to put yourself in a relaxed mental state.
2. Keeping your eyes closed, picture yourself on your mental screen moving toward and achieving your goal—whether it's making a higher income, thinking more positively, or getting along better with people. Keep focusing your thoughts until you can see yourself on your mental screen performing the way you would like to perform.
3. Open your eyes and repeat statements that reaffirm your goal:
"I am confident."
"I am enthusiastic."
"I am important."
"I am in control."
"I am using time effectively."
"I am persistent."
"I am friendly."
"I am achieving my goal."

Keep in mind that visualization is but one important note in your musical repertoire. It is most effective when you use it in conjunction with the other instruments of potential—PMA, productivity, and so on. Think of yourself as a composer trying to blend all the elements of your personality into perfect balance and harmony.

Visualization and Role Playing: Two Examples

Overcoming the Fear of Public Speaking. After using the relaxation technique, imagine that you are on a stage about to give a speech. The curtains are closed, and you can hear the audience quieting down. When the curtains open, you see yourself standing behind the lectern, poised and ready to speak. You are totally self-confident and relaxed, yet formal. The microphone is on the lectern in front of you. A glass of water is on your left. Your notes are on the lectern, but you really don't need them—you can visualize them. You turn them as you speak but that is simply a gesture, because you know your subject dead.

While you are talking, you see faces in the audience displaying interest and warmth. You pause in your talk to take a drink of water. You hear a voice. It is clear, strong, perfectly modulated. It expresses your thoughts clearly and without strain. You feel as though you were talking to an intimate group of friends in your home, and you know you are doing a first-rate job. You feel totally at ease and in harmony with your surroundings.

If you do this exercise once each day for a week or two, your fear of public speaking will gradually disappear. The experience can turn out to be thoroughly enjoyable as well. Try to visualize the setting described above as vividly as you can. If you find this difficult, have someone read the description to you while you mentally "live" it.

Visualizing Congenial Surroundings. Placing yourself in your alpha state, breathe regularly and deeply and begin to count down from 10 to 0. As you feel yourself becoming more and more relaxed, project onto your mental screen a small, cozy room where you feel totally safe and secure. Whenever you enter this room, all fears and apprehensions disappear. As you shut the door, you hear the latch snap into place.

The room, comfortably furnished, contains your favorite

chair. In the far corner is a fireplace. The plush carpeting and the drapes shut out the noise of the outside world, and a soft light enters the room through the window. You feel totally free and relaxed. Cares and worries are not allowed to enter this room. In your retreat you are able to think effortlessly and calmly to solve any problem.

As you practice visualizing this mental retreat, your mind will turn naturally to it for periodic rest. If things get tense, your image of this haven can be a valuable relaxation technique.

■ Activity: Visualizing Success

What would you like to be doing in a specific area a year hence? Imagine, in detail, what it would feel like if you were to achieve this particular goal. Visualize the obstacles that you have overcome. Now visualize your successes, and think of the people who might be associated with you in this effort. Use your mental viewing screen to bring to life the achievement of your goal. ■

■ Activity: "First Aid Kit"

Even the pros need reminding of the basics periodically, so they keep notes to jog their memories and improve their game. Why should you be different?

1. Write your most important goals on a 3" by 5" card.
2. Describe how you will accomplish the goals.
3. Carry the card with you and read it several times a day. ■

Booster Shots

If like most people you find yourself stumbling somewhere along the way, here are some tips to get you going again:

Use triggers. Once you establish a major goal and its necessary subgoals, you must develop triggers—stimuli that will cause you to respond in a manner consistent with your objective. For instance, if your goal is to make more money, a trigger might be a slogan, picture, or saying you post on the wall to remind you of monetary success.

If your goal is to relax and relieve tension, learn to touch your thumb and index finger together as you practice relaxation. This action will soon automatically trigger you to relax.

> Find a trigger for your major goal. If possible, pick a stimulus that occurs early in the morning and frequently throughout the day. And remember—it is extremely important that triggers signal *positive* actions only.

If your goal is to eliminate confusion, try cleaning off the top of your desk every day. This trigger will remind you to tackle just one task at a time.

Use "frequency modification." Vary the frequency of your positive thoughts and actions in accordance with your progress. For example, if you are using vivid visualization once a day and you are not progressing, increase it to two or three times a day.

Increase your intensity. Increase the intensity of the technique you are using. Simply stated, spend more time on setting goals, relaxing, or using any suggestion or exercise in this book. Perhaps your execution is superficial and needs more in-depth treatment. Concentrate, concentrate, concentrate! And follow through.

Taking Stock

It makes sense to take stock of your goals periodically, to find out what it is you want to do with your life and to motivate yourself to follow through with your plans. As you review your goals, you will be accomplishing two important objectives:

1. You will be visualizing your future. It is well known that we think in terms of pictures, but much too often we concentrate on negative images of the past and not enough on important goals for our future (good health, a good marriage, close friends, career success, and so on). The exercise below will stimulate you to think about the things you most enjoy doing, where you want to be in life, and what values are most important to you.

2. You will be pretesting your options before making a major commitment. Much like a geologist taking a sample of the soil, you will be sampling your goals in your mind before immersing yourself in them. Pretesting saves time and costly mistakes: you won't eliminate errors but you will cut down on them. By balancing and coordinating your strategies you are constantly testing your decisions and setting priorities on your goals.

The coordination of goals, behavior, work patterns, and other personal assets is a good and lasting habit. Instead of ignoring your options, making decisions too quickly without regard for all the facts, or being unaware of opportunities, you're ready to respond when the right opportunity arises.

■ Exercise: Listing Your Goals

What are your goals? Spend a few minutes writing them down below. You cannot arrive at a detailed long-range program for your life, so don't try to be too specific with long-term goals. Your purpose is to get a broad picture of what you are looking for in life so you can be prepared to take advantage of whatever comes your way.

You will find that by writing down your goals, you broaden your perspective. Then, by focusing, you will be better able to analyze and update your goals.

1. Begin by listing your long-term goals in the space below. Take into account your career, family, health, financial, personal, and leisure goals. These may be of a general nature at this point. For example, you may wish happiness, success, achievement, recognition, or love. Or, more specifically, you may want to teach, write a book, or continue your education.

_____
_____
_____
_____
_____
_____
_____
_____
_____
_____
_____
_____
_____
_____
_____
_____
_____

2. Next list your goals over the next two to five years. This question will help you refine your long-term goals by narrowing your perspective.

_____
_____
_____
_____
_____
_____
_____
_____
_____

3. Now think about your immediate goals. What do you want to happen over the next six or twelve months? Suppose you had only this year to live. What would you do during the course of the year? Would you continue to live as you are now? Would you quit your job and travel? Would you show more love and affection than you do now? Would you go on a binge?
  If your answers indicate that you are happy and would continue what you are now doing, no major goal changes may be in order. If your answers indicate a different set of values, some real changes may be indicated. List your short-term goals below.

_____
_____
_____
_____
_____
_____
_____
_____
_____

As you work toward the development of your own strategic life plan you are beginning to assemble a considerable amount of information about yourself and your goals. All this information will be useful to you in the final chapter. Assuming you've completed at least some of the exercises, you might evaluate the following questions to see how well you're doing at this point.

1. Are you beginning to get a fix on your skills, your strengths, your achievements? What do you enjoy the most and do the best?
2. Do your answers indicate that you are limiting your options in your life? Are there alternatives you should be considering to enhance the quality of your life?
3. At this point do you know what your most important goals are? Do you emphasize security, power, money, achievement, being popular, or service to others as goals that hold the most meaning for you?
4. Are you beginning to identify those areas that bother you in your career or your life? Do these problems point to external influences (such as your career) or to personal shortcomings?
5. Are you motivated to involve your spouse or confidant in this vital project? If you find it hard to follow through with this project get yourself a partner to help. Make a specific date to meet once a week for a few weeks. Put the date on your calendar. Do it now. It has been said that procrastination has ruined more people than whiskey.

Review: Your Goals

Now that you've completed this section on the second checkpoint of potential, quickly score yourself by answering the following questions using the scale at the bottom of the page.

1. Are your goals clearly defined? ___
2. Are they specific? ___
3. Are they challenging? ___
4. Do you get adequate help from others? ___
5. Do you break goals down into do-able subparts? ___
6. Do you use visualization? ___
7. Can you sustain your goals? ___
8. Do you use triggers and frequency modification? ___
9. Are your goals written down? ___
10. Do you evaluate your progress? ___
11. Do you have a "major" goal? ___
12. Have you done your life planning? ___

Scale

	10	Full use of potential
YES	9	Almost there
	8	Above average
	7	Average
	6	Below average
	5	
NO	4	
	3	Help!
	2	
	1	
	0	

Answer these questions about your responses to the questions above:

    Score 8–10   Am I satisfied?
                          Do I still want to improve?
                          How can I improve?
    Score 6–7   Is this acceptable to me?
                          Is it important to improve?
                          How can I improve?
    Score 5 or below What's happening? Why?
                          Is it important to improve?
                          How can I improve?

If you've identified any areas for improvement, answer the questions below:

    With whom can I discuss this problem?
    Who can give me counsel or direction in solving the problem?
    What step can I take *now* to do something to solve the problem?

Review Notes

Quickly review the marginal notes you have made and the exercises and activities you have done in this section. Summarize your thoughts below.

1. Ideas for follow-up developed as you read this section:

   _____
   _____
   _____
   _____

2. Ideas you believe should be included in your coordinated action plan:

   _____
   _____
   _____
   _____
   _____

3. Thoughts that occur to you at this time about
    (a) Setting goals within the proper guidelines (clarity, realism, time limits):

    _____
    _____
    _____
    _____
    _____

    (b) Using personal rewards to help you achieve your goals:

    _____
    _____
    _____
    _____
    _____

    (c) Using visualization as a tool in setting goals:

    _____
    _____
    _____
    _____
    _____

    (d) Using triggers, frequency modification, and increased intensity:

    _____
    _____
    _____
    _____
    _____

4. Other thoughts:

    _____
    _____
    _____
    _____
    _____

Additional Reading

One action step available to help you improve is to learn more about an area suggested in this section. Here is a list of books you might consider for additional study:

The Success Factor by Robert Sharpe. New York: Warner Books, 1976.

Choosing Success by Dorothy Jongeward and Philip Seyer. New York: John Wiley & Son, 1978.

Yes, You Can! by Art Linkletter. New York: Simon & Schuster, 1979.

Passages by Gail Sheehy. New York: Bantam Books, 1977.

The Three Boxes of Life by Richard N. Bolles. Berkeley: Ten Speed Press, 1978.

The Seasons of a Man's Life by Daniel J. Levinson. New York: Ballantine Books, 1978.

Success by Michael Korda. New York: Ballantine Books, 1978.

Guide to Developing Your Potential by Herbert A. Otto. Hollywood, Calif.: Wilshire Book Co., 1973.

SECTION IV

Checkpoint 3: Your Self-Image

The rational, mature human being begins each day by confronting the self he really is, accepting that self for what it is, and then takes the next step toward becoming a full and whole human being. He seeks to expand his value not only to others but, more important, to himself.
—G. H. Russell and Kenneth Black, Jr.
Human Behavior in Business

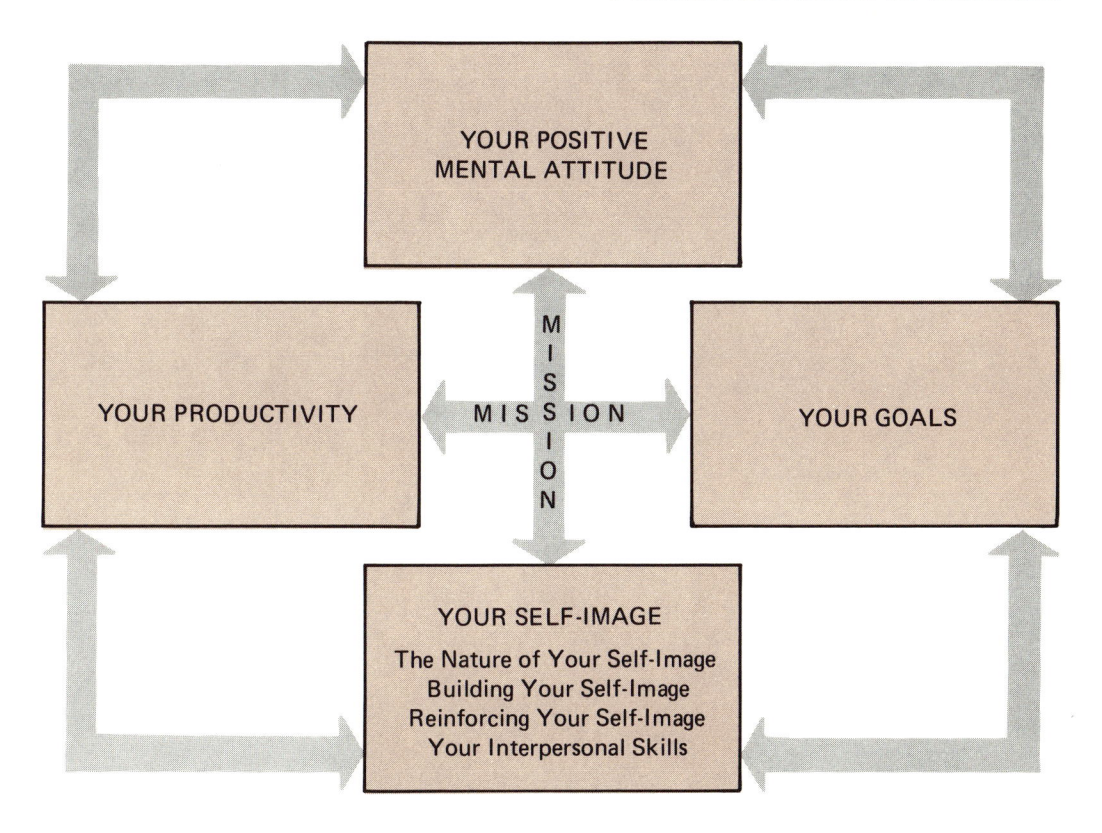

```
                    ┌─────────────────────┐
                    │   YOUR POSITIVE     │
                    │  MENTAL ATTITUDE    │
                    └─────────────────────┘
                              │
                              M
                              I
                              S
                              S
┌──────────────────┐   I              ┌──────────────┐
│ YOUR PRODUCTIVITY│ ← MISSION →      │  YOUR GOALS  │
└──────────────────┘   O              └──────────────┘
                              N
                              │
                    ┌─────────────────────┐
                    │   YOUR SELF-IMAGE   │
                    │ The Nature of Your Self-Image │
                    │ Building Your Self-Image │
                    │ Reinforcing Your Self-Image │
                    │ Your Interpersonal Skills │
                    └─────────────────────┘
```

9. The Nature of Your Self-Image

One of the great impediments to personal progress is the feeling "I don't think I can do it." Realistically there are many things in life that you cannot do without training—for example, playing a musical instrument, keeping a set of books, flying an airplane, or practicing medicine. But more often it is not lack of training that holds back full commitment—it's the false feeling "I can't." Even though you may be proficient at a sport or in your work, you may "freeze" at critical moments because of a poor self-image. It is at these moments that the self-image acts as a barrier to progress.

Much has been written about the all-important self-image. What are the basic facts?

1. The self-image is constantly at work in all facets of your life:

> "I'm not attractive."
> "I really can play the violin."
> "I'm a born loser."
> "I'm a good person."
> "I'm not confident of myself."

2. These "images" of how you will perform or how you value yourself begin at birth. They are based on your reactions to your environment, your experiences with parents and teachers, your earliest achievements, and so on. This information is recorded in your subconscious for future use, much as a computer stores information for future retrieval. Your "mental computer" retains your fears, prejudices, successes, and failures. These events cannot be erased.

3. Your computer functions automatically. It works on the information you give it. In computer language it's "garbage in–garbage out," but it can just as well be "success in–success out."

4. Your computer is "cybernetic"—it is programmed to seek your goals automatically. It moves toward the target and corrects

course as though it were a guided missile launched by a ship. The most common illustration of this occurs when you "sleep on a problem" and somehow have the answer the next morning.

■ Activity: Control Your Built-In Computer

1. Decide now to take control of your self-image. See yourself at the control panel of your built-in computer. Feed it the right material.
2. Begin to program your computer with positive, exciting goals. Don't try to change previously stored material—that is permanently locked in. Instead, make new programs or recordings of your objectives as developed throughout this book.
3. Coordinate your skills and assets so you can effectively set priorities for your goals and develop the plans to achieve them. ■

The Importance of Your Self-Image

So important is the self-concept that many experts rank it second only to survival among basic human drives. It is a powerful influence that determines happiness, health, effectiveness, relations with others—even the will to live. If you think you're unimportant, chances are you'll be unimportant. If you think you're a big deal, you may well be a big deal. Your actions will tend to support your claims, at least over the long haul.

Those who achieve are often so confident of their own abilities that they convince others of their superiority. And they sometimes achieve much more than their true ability warrants. A strong self-image and achievement go hand in hand—one feeds on the other. While true talent cannot be created, it can be greatly nurtured where it exists. The confidence created by small successes can "prime the pump" and turn loose a flood of further achievements.

Many people who occupy positions of leadership are in reality no brighter and no more decisive, alert, and informed than many of those they command. Is the president of your firm the smartest person in your company? Not likely. The difference may be one of image rather than raw ability.

Here is what several people have had to say about the importance of a strong self-image:

A company president was asked what he felt was the difference between himself and those who had failed to keep pace with him. "That's easy," he said. "I have a better opinion of myself. Fifteen years ago I already saw myself sitting in this chair. There was no doubt in my mind I would make it. When I started visualizing myself as company president, I began to dress and act in a manner that was consistent with being company president. I had self-confidence. I knew I could do it."

General R. E. Chambers, former chief of the Army's psychiatry division, said, "Many potential heroes, both men and women, live out their lives in deep doubt. If they only knew they had these deep resources, it would help give them the self-reliance to meet most problems, even a big crisis."

Peter Engel, president of the Helena Rubinstein Company, said "It is typical of the achiever that he has concentrated upon his strengths until they have overcome his weaknesses and have become the essence of who he is."

Self-Acceptance

An important part of building a strong self-image is learning to accept yourself. Once you do, acceptance by others is no longer a matter of life or death. When you accept the "real you," many good things happen. You become secure within yourself, gain peace of mind, release your tensions, and boost your self-confidence. You become the best "you" that's ever been made—one of a kind, in mint condition. As Shakespeare said, "This above all, to thine own self be true. And it must follow as the night the day, thou canst not then be false to any man." Once you accept yourself for your true worth, false feelings of inferiority will gradually disappear.

Connie Mack, manager of the old Philadelphia Athletics, said, "I have seen boys on my baseball team go into slumps and never come out of them. And I have seen others snap right back better than ever. I guess more players defeat themselves than are ever licked by an opposing team. The first thing any man has to know is how to handle himself."

Emile Coué once said, "Every day in every way I'm getting better and better." You may be getting better at your work, at a hobby, or at being a better citizen. You may be more loving, wiser, or healthier. Some of your friends may be smarter than

> When you accept yourself as a person, you have made major progress in climbing your mountain. How do you get to be more at ease with yourself? How do you stop questioning your own worth or the need to "prove" your own worth? You remove this important obstacle to growth when you recognize that *who you are doesn't change.* You came in the world the way you are and you're going out that way.

you, make more money than you, or play a better game of golf. The question is: Are these people better or worse than you? Obviously, they are neither. Your worth as a person is not determined by any one set of characteristics or skills. Self-accepting people don't look down on some of their associates while standing in awe of others. They accept others in terms of their basic worth as human beings.

The Payoff of Self-Acceptance

- When you accept yourself as you are, you no longer need to prove yourself. You recognize that you are neither inferior nor superior, that you are just you. Dismiss any thoughts of inferiority and superiority; laugh them off as unworthy.
- With true self-acceptance, you don't sit in judgment of yourself. You have eliminated the need to question your own worth. You are no longer like the proverbial puppy chasing its own tail. Instead, like the setter, you move straight to the target. You don't dwell on your mistakes.
- When you can accept yourself, you feel good about yourself. Setting and pursuing goals becomes more pleasurable, and even mediocre results provide feedback, not disgrace. Self-acceptance is definitely a stress-releasing philosophy.
- Because you no longer labor under the burden of proving yourself, you are free to choose your course of action and to experience the fulfillment of living, achieving, and participating without the burdens of negativism ("I can't do it") or compulsiveness ("I must do it").

Self-acceptance is the cornerstone of your self-esteem. It provides an inner sense of peace and relaxation and a sense of fulfillment because you're not at war with yourself. It helps you live with yourself and enables you to accept other people. This freedom, this fulfillment stimulates your growth and achievement.

■ Exercise: Boosting Your Image

1. Take out a picture of yourself that you like. Why do you like this picture?

   _____
   _____
   _____
   _____
   _____

2. Describe some of your personal characteristics that are pleasing to you.

   _____
   _____
   _____
   _____
   _____

3. What goals and ideals do you have that make you feel good?

   _____
   _____
   _____
   _____
   _____

4. Describe something you enjoy doing and do well.

   _____
   _____
   _____
   _____
   _____

5. Describe something about your physical self that you like.

   _____
   _____
   _____
   _____
   _____

■

Your Career Self-Image

Just as you have an image of yourself as a private person (spouse, parent, friend), so you have an image of yourself as a professional in your career. This image is vital to career success or failure. For example, a salesman who does not believe a prospect will buy his product is unlikely to make the sale. He will unconsciously project this image by his lack of enthusiasm and by his self-consciousness about asking for the order. In any career—professional athletics, law, medicine—a person will act like the type of person he believes himself to be. The loser will often find some way to fail, in spite of his best intentions and even if good fortune is handed to him on a platter. The success-oriented person will achieve, grow, and win despite the odds. He is literally "primed" for success.

> *Ah, but a man's reach should exceed his grasp—or what's a heaven for?*
> —Robert Browning

How do you view your current performance? What do you see as your potential for career growth? The two columns below illustrate how you might evaluate yourself now and where you would like to be a year from now?

	Today	A Year from Now	
	10	10	
	9	9	———
	8	8	Effective Range
———	7	7	———
Effective Range	6	6	
———	5	5	
	4	4	
	3	3	
	2	2	
	1	1	
	0	0	

Note that the term "effective range" is used, because the self-image is a variable, operating within limits. Your effective range at work can change from day to day because of business conditions, competitive pressures, the boss's disposition, the volume of work, and so forth. The limits of your effective range are based on two factors: your real abilities, and what you think of your abilities.

Changing your career effective range is an unusually difficult goal. It means, in part:

1. Seeing yourself operating in the improved range before it happens.
2. Acting out your new role through visualization and role playing so you "preview" what is to come.
3. Analyzing each checkpoint—PMA, goals, self-image, and productivity—to determine areas that need work.
4. Coming up with an action program that coordinates your assets effectively.

Self-Confidence and the Self-Image

Self-confidence and a strong self-image go hand in hand. One of the best illustrations of this is in the sales field. Ninety-nine percent of the time when salespeople lack self-confidence, it is not because they lack ability. It is usually because they measure themselves by an unrealistic standard. This standard is gen-

> *Self-Confidence or Self-Importance?*
>
> A member of President Lincoln's cabinet received a letter from a woman in Ohio. In it she asked a small favor for her young son. The new official, unduly puffed up with his own importance, replied, "Dear Madam: I am now so busy with the affairs of the nation that I have no time for the problems of the individual."
>
> The old woman, unimpressed by his high station, took her quill in hand and responded, "So far the Almighty ain't been that busy."

erally the image of an outstandingly successful salesperson with a dynamite personality and a "can't miss" approach. This character never fails and is never discouraged. Everyone likes him. He is clever and debonair, dynamic and attractive.

The truth is there are no such salespeople. Each year the life insurance industry's most successful agents gather at meetings of the "Million Dollar Roundtable." These people are a cross-section of the population—short and tall, fat and lean, attractive and unattractive. They are alike only in the outstanding results they produce.

In a study of 600 sales representatives, the Minnesota Mining and Manufacturing Company sought to determine what set the successes apart from the failures. The difference was not one of talent, personality, or even intelligence. The successes simply thought of themselves as *good* salespeople—the failures did not. The successful group's opinions of their abilities and talents were closer to their own standards of success.

> The basis for your actions is rooted in the picture you hold of yourself, of your relationships with others, and of your environment. This picture is your self-image. Everything you see or do will relate to it. If you picture yourself as harassed and at the mercy of forces beyond your control, you will act in accordance with this image. If you picture yourself as confident and more than a match for any situation, you will do the things that correspond with that image.

■ Exercise: Testing Your Self-Confidence

In the space below, list what you consider to be your strongest points, even your minor strengths. Then list all your weaknesses.

Strengths	Weaknesses
_____	_____
_____	_____
_____	_____
_____	_____
_____	_____
_____	_____
_____	_____
_____	_____
_____	_____
_____	_____

If you have listed more strengths than weaknesses you tend to be self-confident and self-assured. If you have listed more weaknesses, you probably don't understand your full potential. It's not because you actually have more weak than strong points—it's because you *think* your flaws outweigh your talents. And you are probably too self-conscious about your flaws.

Remember, your picture of yourself dictates your success in your work as well as in your personal life. Once your self-image is formed (usually at an early age), it is not easily modified, no matter how far it may depart from reality. The important thing to remember is that it *can* be changed—through persistent effort. ■

10. Building Your Self-Image

The self-image is an exceptionally valuable tool in realizing potential. Yet few people use their picture of themselves in a thoughtful, positive way. You will doubtless acknowledge that you have some picture of yourself, but you probably do not know what that self really is or how it influences your actions.

Rating Your Self-Esteem

How do you really feel about yourself? What are your deep-down feelings of personal worth and significance? How high (or low) is your self-esteem? Here are some typical unspoken thoughts illustrating both ends of the self-esteem spectrum:

Low Self-Esteem Talk	*High Self-Esteem Talk*
"I'm not sure of my abilities."	"I am worthy of respect."
"I don't expect much from myself."	"I believe I have a good idea of what is right."
"Something's wrong with everything I do."	"I do high-quality work."
"I expect things to get worse."	"I like myself as a person."

If you are like most people, you could use a much higher

> Your self-esteem forms the basis for your positive mental attitude. The moment you begin to raise your self-esteem a notch you also begin to release your potential. You not only start meeting your goals more easily; you also start having more fun achieving them.

self-esteem rating. If yours is high, good for you! But suppose it's low or somewhere in the middle. Using a 0-to-10 scale, rate yourself:

	10
High self-esteem	9
	8
	7
Average self-esteem	6
	5
	4
	3
Low self-esteem	2
	1
	0

Bear in mind that your rating may be temporarily affected by outside conditions, such as your office or home situation. These outside factors can get you up or down, but generally for short periods of time. Otherwise, there is a basic level of self-esteem that you carry with you at all times. You get a hint of it each morning when you look in the mirror and greet yourself with "Hi there, good-looking." Or maybe it's "What are you looking at me for, turkey?" A norm emerges over the years, over many tubes of toothpaste. Wherever your self-esteem rests now, of course, your job is to push it higher.

What can you do to raise your self-esteem just one notch higher—and build a greater sense of personal worth? Here are a few tips:

Build your self-esteem just before going to sleep at night. The mental images you conjure up just before sleep will most likely be replayed and reinforced during sleep. The effect is a profound one. Instead of fretting over problems, use the minutes before sleep to flood your mind with positive thoughts about yourself and your achievements. If you really want to do a first-class job tape-record the positive ideas in this book as well as personal achievements that have been meaningful to you. Listen to the tape every night for a month or two just before you retire. The program can have dynamic results.

Visualize those times when you really felt good about yourself. Practice boosting your self-esteem with the same dedication you would devote to any skill you wished to develop, such as playing a musical instrument or learning to program a computer. Re-create in your imagination those times when you really felt good about you. When you are relaxing think about times when you felt the most worthwhile. Perhaps you made a good presentation, or spent time with a loved one. Build your esteem to the point where you can say with sincerity, "I like the kind of person I am. I feel good about myself and I enjoy living with myself."

Build the self-esteem of other people. There is a great truth in the adage "The more you give the more you get." In each of your relationships—with your spouse, your child, a co-worker, a friend—you send messages that either enhance or diminish the other person. You cannot help but reinforce your own self-esteem when you let others know that you value their worth.

How do you build the self-esteem of other people?

You tell them you love them, if indeed you do.
You listen to what they are saying.
You express genuine feelings you have about them.
You convey your interest by words and actions.

Assessing Your Strengths

Obviously, an important part of strengthening your self-image is to discover all you can about the subject—you. At the outset you must decide whether you are for yourself or against yourself. You can live a life of constantly putting yourself down when you should be lifting yourself up. You can be your own best friend or your own worst enemy. Remember, there will always be pain and trouble and loss in life. Don't let negatives destroy you. In strengthening your self-image, you must capitalize on your good qualities.

Few people ever appeared to have as much going for them as the late Marilyn Monroe. In a few short years she achieved fame, wealth, professional success, and public adulation. It would be difficult to devise a more sensational success story or public image. Then one night in August 1962 another image of Marilyn Monroe—her own—was drawn into bold relief. Her suicide reflected a deeply troubled woman who felt isolated, used, unfulfilled, and unloved. Her final act of self-destruction gave shocking testimony to her inner torment.

The business world carefully studies the profitability of its products. It strengthens and promotes the most profitable products and drops the weak ones. In the same way, you should be identifying and reinforcing your own skills and strengths. The right combination makes you valuable to your employer and "alive" to others and to yourself.

Pause for a moment to take stock of yourself. What makes you tick? What are your strengths? Your achievements? Your sources of pride? As you assess your abilities:

1. Concentrate on your uniqueness and excellence.
2. Recognize that you have many demonstrated achievements in your lifetime.
3. Keep in mind that identifying your strengths helps you take charge of your life. It emphasizes your strong points as the basis of your self-image and helps point up the interaction between your strengths and weaknesses. For example, weakness in one area (health) may cause a strong area (work) to break down.

The following self-evaluation questionnaire can help you take the measure of your sense of personal worth.

Self-Evaluation: Inventory of Personal Strengths

1. Think back over your life and recall experiences that reflect your personality. Check the words below that seem to describe you:

☐ Honest	☐ Thorough	☐ Hardworking
☐ Loyal	☐ Enthusiastic	☐ Reliable
☐ Compassionate	☐ Goal-oriented	☐ Persistent
☐ Cooperative	☐ Intelligent	☐ Confident
☐ Sense of humor	☐ Sociable	☐ Open-minded
☐ Cheerful	☐ Creative	☐ Disciplined
☐ Calm	☐ Willing	☐ Realistic
☐ Relaxed	☐ Good-natured	☐ Positive
☐ Competitive	☐ Vigorous	☐ Attractive
	☐ Peaceful	

Write down areas you feel might need work. For example, if you are not enthusiastic you may want to work on developing this important quality.

_____

_____

_____

_____

2. Write down your strengths and achievements in the areas listed below. Some ideas are given for starters.

Career (setting goals, job satisfaction, career decisions, pride in work, use of time, enjoyment of work, taking responsibility, reaching goals, making decisions)

_____
_____
_____
_____

Health (medical checkups, physical well-being, nutrition, mental attitude)

_____
_____
_____
_____

Physical Activity (exercise, outdoor activities, camping, golf, tennis, bowling)

_____
_____
_____
_____

Organizational Strengths (organizing projects or clubs, developing and achieving goals, carrying out orders, leadership qualities)

_____
_____
_____
_____

Hobbies and Crafts (photography, reading, carpentry, music)

_____
_____
_____
_____

Education (advanced study, special courses, on-the-job training, self-study)

_____
_____
_____
_____

Special Aptitudes (mechanical ability, sales ability, skill with hands, creative thinking)

_____
_____
_____
_____

Strength Through Others (relationships with spouse, children, relatives, friends, associates)

_____
_____
_____
_____

Intellectual Strengths (intellectual curiosity, willingness to accept new ideas, enjoyment of learning, reading)

_____
_____
_____
_____

Creative Strengths (developing new ideas in relation to your home, family, job, avocation)

_____
_____
_____
_____

Esthetic Strengths (enjoying the beauty of music, nature, and art; improving your surroundings)

_____
_____
_____
_____

Spiritual Strengths (church membership, feeling close to God, expressing moral and religious values in living, living what you believe)

_____
_____
_____
_____

Financial Management (ability to earn money, living within your income, financial growth)

_____
_____
_____
_____

3. You are now ready to assess your potential for growth. Go over your comments above and look for patterns. Pay special attention to activities you enjoy—career hobbies, travel, and so forth. What particularly interests you? What have people

praised you for? What have been your major achievements? Use the space below to assess your potential for personal growth.

11. Reinforcing Your Self-Image

Role Playing

Your ability to make your self-image work for you is critical to realizing your potential. However, *feeling* successful before you *are* successful can be difficult and takes a bit of discipline. You can help develop your self-image by playing your "role" properly. Life is indeed a stage, and nowhere is this more evident than in the Marine Corps. When Marine reservists put on that uniform, they change. They stand taller, they become more confident, and they exude authority.

What is your concept of your role? Who and what do you truly represent? What are your sources of pride and accomplishment? For example, if you were a salesman, you might see your role in these terms:

"I am a professional salesman for a great company."

"I have a great product and service that the customer is unlikely to get elsewhere."

■ *Exercise: Defining Your Role*

In the space below write down your concept of your role—who and what you feel you represent.

_____
_____
_____
_____

Copy this statement on a 3" by 5" card and carry it with you. Refer to it constantly until your role becomes a natural extension of your personality. ■

■ Activity: Play Your Role

1. Keep thinking about the successes you *intend* to achieve in your role.
2. Spend a few minutes several times a day getting your attitudes in order. Concentrate on your need to believe in yourself, your enthusiasm, and your self-image.
3. Prepare yourself to welcome all your daily problems as challenges. ■

■ Activity: Act Out Other Roles

Suppose you were your boss or the chairman of a particular committee. Play out their behaviors in your mind—fantasize. This can help you develop new strengths or detect hidden ones. It may even give you a new direction altogether. ■

Building a "Success" Frame of Mind

One of the most important assets in your success repertoire is your ability to change your beliefs, your mental picture of yourself, so you can unlock your hidden talents and abilities. This doesn't mean you change yourself. It means that you make the most of what you already have. Most of us have a lot more going for us than we realize, and we're much more competent than we give ourselves credit for being. Building a success attitude is much like clearing the decks on board ship; we must sweep away negative debris we have accumulated about ourselves over the years. These false and limiting self-images hinder our ability to achieve our goals. They are spoilers—of happiness, achievement, and personal fulfillment.

> *People do not lack strength. They lack will.*
> —Victor Hugo

The techniques described below can help you go a long way toward strengthening your self-image and building a success frame of mind. You may smile at these techniques as being too simple, too unsophisticated. Don't believe it. Success comes from any number of simple approaches such as these. You cannot afford to disregard any of them. You don't have to do them all, but at least give them a try and see what works for you.

Cheerleading: All Right! The person who is half-alive needs to be resold on himself. A friend of mine, John Mahoney, uses the following technique several times a day with excellent results. He constantly refers to what he calls his "Wheaties card," which gives him the following commercial:

"John, I want you to meet the best friend you have, John Mahoney. John, you are the greatest. You've got great ability and you should go first class all the way.

"John, you believe in happiness, inner peace, people, and your work.

"You're enthusiastic, John. You look good, feel good, and every day you're getting better.

"John, put your drive and desire to live better to work for you. Remember this—nothing can stop you!"

Mirror, Mirror. Many great salesmen, orators, and actors have used the mirror to perfect their technique. For example, Winston Churchill never made an important speech without practicing it before a mirror. Using the mirror helps you create the image you want others to see. You also get a better handle on your self-image and strengthen its hold on your mind.

■ Activity: The Mirror Technique

Stand in front of a mirror. Breathe deeply three or four times and hold yourself erect until you feel a sense of power and strength. Look deeply into your eyes and tell yourself you are going to get what you want. Say it out loud and practice doing it twice a day. On the mirror post slogans and sayings that support your goal. ■

You Are What You Read. Dr. David McClelland of Harvard University, a noted researcher in achievement, analyzed the reading material of the general population. He found that when the literature was success-oriented and optimistic, achievement levels were high. When the literature was pessimistic or depicted people as victims of circumstance, achievement levels were low. Thus it seems that achievement-oriented literature can help people think in terms of goals and success. It can be most supportive to the development of a healthy self-image.

■ Activity: Read About Success

1. Select reading material that is goal-oriented and achievement-oriented. For example, read a biography this month of someone at the top of your field, sport, or hobby.
2. Try to do some of this type of reading every day. As you read, imagine yourself achieving accomplishments similar to those of the person you are reading about. ■

Self-Stroking. Self-stroking means taking pride and pleasure in yourself and your achievements. It means consciously patting yourself on the back for the good things you have done; doing things that give you joy instead of pain; having compassion for yourself; and recognizing yourself for your good works and appreciating your blessings. Your feelings for yourself are the key to your happiness and peace of mind.

Even though external stroking, or praise from others, can be an important factor in mental outlook, more often than not it cannot be depended upon. In today's world good performance is *expected*, if not always praised. But we can always praise ourselves. We know how we perform, even if no one else does.

Don't hesitate to reward yourself for a job well done. If you complete a project on time and under budget, have a night on the town with your spouse or have a special dinner or weekend. To others, you simply did what you were supposed to do. To you, you "busted a gut" to get the job done and made it look easy. Tell yourself how much you appreciated the effort. This will keep you going despite the lack of external stroking.

Money and Your Self-Image

It is critical that you realistically appraise your attitude toward money. In his book *Think Rich*, H. Stanley Judd points out that many people throw away a lifetime of opportunities because they "feel poor." Realistically you may be short of cash, but inside you can be brimming over with joy, optimism, and energy.

Most of us live pretty well in this society. Undreamed of luxuries are now within our reach. Products from around the world, libraries full of books, elegant parks, sports stadiums, and excellent restaurants—these are only a few of the opportunities and pleasures available.

If, in spite of these luxuries, your outlook on life is clouded by persistent feelings of "poverty," money will always push you around, no matter how much you have. *Feeling* poor will restrict your potential to live life on better terms. Each time you become depressed because you envy someone or long for something you don't have, you will experience a feeling of insecurity. You become a prisoner of money. Don't surrender. Instead, develop a healthy attitude toward money. Here's how:

Don't let money rule your life. Make the most of what you have now, and plan to get the most out of whatever you may acquire.

Value yourself. You are Numero Uno. Your standards are your own, not someone else's, and you contribute to the best of your ability.

Value what you have more than you value what other people have. Decide that whatever your situation is right now, you will live your life with the same peace of mind that often comes with wealth.

Use your imagination. Lock up negative thoughts and atti-

Two millionaires lost everything in the 1929 stock market crash. One leaped out of his office window; the other left for six months to fish in Canada. Same problem—two solutions.

> Begin to think and act *as if* money were no longer a problem in your life. Whatever your situation, you can live your life with the same peace of mind that wealth often brings.

tudes about money. Look at money as a resource rather than a problem. Don't play the "money security game." Be content and secure now. Remember that the richness of life does not depend on how much money you make. Your true wealth lies in personal growth, friendships, health, love, service, and happiness.

Live within your means. Ben Franklin said, "A happy person makes $100 a week and spends $99. An unhappy person makes $100 a week and spends $101." Overspending can change your attitude and self-image fast.

> *O money, money, money*
> *I am not necessarily one of those who think thee holy.*
> *But I often stop to wonder*
> *how thou canst go out so fast when thou comest in so slowly.*
>
> —Ogden Nash

Toward a Realistic Self-Image

Improving your self-image does not necessarily mean becoming something you're not. It does mean changing your mental picture of yourself if the current edition is not doing you justice.

Strengthening your self-image will not automatically give you new abilities or powers, but it can release the potential which you perhaps lacked the confidence to exploit. Remember, you cannot change a poor self-image by willpower alone. You must justify the change. It's got to be credible to you. You must realize that a new image is both necessary and appropriate.

You cannot begin to realize your potential if you deny your

own uniqueness, dislike yourself, and fail to recognize your own worth. "It is the young man of little faith who says, 'I am nothing.'" said Edward Bok. "It is the young man of true conception who says, 'I am everything,' and then goes on to prove it. That does not spell conceit or egotism and if people think so, let them think so. Enough for us to know it means faith, trust, confidence, the human expression of God within us. He says 'Do my work!' Go and do it. No matter what it is. Do it, but do it with zest, a keenness, a gusto that surmounts obstacles and brushes aside discouragement."

Finally, from a practical standpoint, take a good look at some of the outward manifestations of your self-image: your clothes, automobile, house, garden, desk, and all the many physical expressions of you. Make a list of the things that need improvement and go to work on them this weekend.

Self-Image, Goals, and Values

Your self-image and goals are inextricably bound to the values that are important to you. These values cover a wide range—money, power, service to others, physical fitness, cultural pursuits.

Your mix of values is unique to you. These values determine how you spend your time before, during, and after the workday. Think, for instance, how you'd spend portions of your day if you considered being with your children of primary importance. You'd probably have to rearrange your schedule. You might have to work fewer hours. Or you might have to start working earlier in the day to find more time for the children. Your goals become more obvious and meaningful when you analyze your entire value system.

To make your life planning program effective, it is important that you identify all your values. Consider your true feelings about money, leisure, career, health, and so on. Bringing these values into focus will help you decide what you really want out of life.

The following self-evaluation questionnaire raises several important issues about your value system. It covers your career, family, health, personality, finances, and use of leisure time. As you work through the questions, you will become more aware of the importance you have been placing on each of these areas.

Score yourself on each question using a scale of 0 to 10 (where 0 represents "extreme dissatisfaction" and 10 represents "extreme satisfaction"). After you have answered every question in each section, review your responses one at a time. Ask yourself, "Am I really satisfied with the answer?"

Self-Evaluation: Career Development. Career development and career satisfaction are fundamental in coordinating your assets. The career person is indeed climbing a mountain. In answering the questions below, try to evaluate how you can make your climb more profitable and enjoyable.

Do I have career goals? ___

Are they clear and realistic? ___

Do they mean a great deal to me? ___

Do I like my career? ___

Do I study work-related materials? ___

Am I enthusiastic about my work? ___

Am I fully committed to my career? _____

Do I try to give more time to the job than is required? _____

Am I reasonably well rewarded for my work? _____

Do I manage myself effectively? _____

Do I get along with my boss? _____

Do I need further education? _____

Am I becoming obsolete? _____

Should I consider a job change? _____

Do outside interests conflict with my career? _____

Are there other questions I need to consider in the area of career development?

_____

_____

_____

_____

Self-Evaluation: Family Development. Certainly your family is important to you. So important, in fact, that if you do not give family life the proper attention, your fulfillment in all other areas of your life may be jeopardized.

Do I still love my spouse? _____

Does my spouse still love me? _____

Does my mate have the same goals I have? _____

Do I ever bring home a gift as a spontaneous gesture of affection? _____

Do I make a conscious effort to improve my marital relationship? _____

Do I spend enough time with my family? _____

Does my family want to spend time with me? _____

Do I adequately provide for my family's material needs? _____

Do I provide moral and spiritual guidance? _____

Is my family happy? _____

Do vacations meet the needs of each family member? _____

Do I love my children? ___

Are there other questions I need to consider in the area of family development?

_____
_____
_____
_____
_____

Self-Evaluation: Health. Are you giving your health the time and attention it deserves? It is your most important asset and affects your ability to achieve your goals and to derive pleasure out of life.

Have I had a checkup lately? ___

Do I have a good energy level? ___

Am I overweight? ___

Do I get enough exercise? ___

Do I drink too much? ___

Do I smoke too much? ___

Is my nutrition good? ___

Am I getting proper rest? ___

Is stress affecting my health? ___

Is my sex life good? ___

Am I proud of my physical condition? ___

Is my heart and lung response adequate to meet the energy needs of daily living? ___

Are there other questions I need to consider in the area of health?

_____
_____
_____
_____
_____

Self-Evaluation: Personality Development. Your personality plays a major role in determining your success. An analysis of your personality style is an important factor in your personal growth.

Do I really like people? ___
Do other people really like me? ___
Am I outgoing in social situations? ___
Do others listen when I'm talking? ___
Do I have a group of very close friends? ___
Am I an active member of a community group? ___
Do I speak well before groups? ___
Am I proud of myself? ___
Do I talk interestingly? ___
Do I empathize well? ___

Are there other questions I need to consider in the area of personality development?

_____
_____
_____
_____
_____

Self-Evaluation: Financial Development. Most of us consider wealth a yardstick for measuring success. Yet deep inside we know that true success lies in achieving our lifetime goals and realizing our potential. Nevertheless, financial development may well be the means by which many other goals are achieved. You should now consider it carefully in that light.

Do I give serious consideration to my financial progress? ___
Has my income increased at a satisfactory pace? ___
Do I expect my income to increase significantly over the next year or so? ___
Am I willing to "pay the price" for financial success? ___

Am I living within my current income?   ___

Are installment payments taking too much of my income? ___

Could I save a significant amount of money by making some change in my purchasing policies? ___

Do I have a planned savings or investment program? ___

Is this program increasing annually? ___

Can I improve the program? ___

Could I meet all my financial obligations if I were unable to work? ___

Do I have a good credit rating? ___

Are there other questions I need to consider in the area of financial development?

_____

_____

_____

_____

Self-Evaluation: Leisure and Recreation. Leisure time coordinates especially well with stress release, career growth, retirement planning, intellectual growth, and sheer pleasure. Leisure activities can have a meaning all their own or they can be a pleasurable extension of other facets of life.

Do I use my leisure time well? ___

Is my leisure time a pleasurable extension of my career? ___

Can I relax and do nothing? ___

Do I enjoy sharing my leisure time with others? ___

Do I use recreation time to improve my health? ___

Do I overschedule my leisure and recreational time? ___

Do I thoroughly enjoy my leisure time? ___

Am I developing leisure activities that will last all my life? ___

Do I have a fulfilling hobby? ___

124 Are there other questions I need to consider in the area of leisure and recreation?

12. Your Interpersonal Skills

The ability to communicate effectively plays a vital role in successful living. In your career it can mean success or failure, and in your personal life it can spell the difference between happiness and misery. Most of life is spent in self-communication. We think and converse with ourselves daily. We talk ourselves into doing something—or out of wanting something. Whether we talk to ourselves positively or negatively has a profound effect on our self-image.

There is a feedback effect between self-talk and communication with others, similar to the mental and physical feedback cycle that occurs with stress. Stated briefly, positive self-talk leads to positive communication with others; positive communication with others leads to positive self-talk.

The golden rule tells us, "Do unto others as you would have them do unto you." People have a basic need to have their judgments confirmed—to feel that their opinions are in accord with those of others. Because of this, if you do agree with other people, even if it's only about the weather, let them know it. We all like pleasant people and shy away from those who are disagreeable.

> Successful people constantly practice positive self-talk and positive conversation with others. They practice truly effective communications, aware of the fact that interpersonal relationships are won or lost in the first few minutes of conversation.

The important point is this: The more you agree with another person, the more agreement he or she will give you. Psychologists have found that people feel compelled to "give what they get." This law of return on what you communicate works with everybody—husbands, wives, children, executives, customers. If you give others what they want, they will be more inclined to give you what you want. "Agree with thine adversary quickly while thou are in the way with him," says the Bible.

Just before General George C. Marshall sent H. H. (Hap) Arnold to the Southwest Pacific as commander of the U.S. Air Force, he said: "I'd like to make three suggestions about carrying out your responsibilities of leadership out there: (1) Listen to the other fellow's story, (2) don't get mad, and (3) let the other fellow tell his story first." Using this advice, General Arnold became one of the most popular and accomplished leaders of World War II.

All highly successful salespeople apply the golden rule of two-way communication. They ask questions, seek opinions, make rewarding statements, and paraphrase the other person's views in an effort to provide "positive feedback." The more support the salesman gives the prospect, the more friendly and interested the prospect becomes. Soon both salesman and prospect feel as if they know and understand each other well. A "we" attitude takes over—and everyone is more receptive to ideas from "we" than to those from "they."

Many old-fashioned selling methods can be of substantial value in daily communications. For example, a hearty handshake, a sincere smile, and a warm greeting are all well received by others. Research has shown that gestures and comments that might otherwise seem insignificant can powerfully influence another person's opinion. Nodding your head in agreement, leaning forward in a chair to show interest, smiling, and simply

---

We reproach people for talking about themselves; but it is the subject they treat best.
—Anatole France

saying "Fine" or "That's good" are important to effective communication.

The Art of Listening

You can do wonders for your self-image and your ability to communicate if you learn the art of listening. Do you really listen when someone is talking? Listening, *really listening*, has a tremendous psychological value. Here's how you can become a better listener:

1. Lean slightly forward in your chair when you are talking to someone. Anticipate two-way communication.
2. Set your mental machinery to "receive" rather than to "broadcast." Look concerned. Better yet, *be* concerned.
3. Don't be tempted to think about what you are going to say next.

The "we" feeling is generated by asking questions and soliciting opinions. Real two-way communication is based on respect for the other person's views. Try to get others to talk about themselves. How do they feel? What are they interested in? What are they doing with their time? How is their job going? These are all areas in which people are expert. There is definite value in encouraging others to talk about themselves. Call it getting them off on an "ego trip." No matter what the subject or topic may be, all of us ultimately talk about ourselves.

> *Blessed are they who have nothing to say, and who cannot be persuaded to say it.*
> —James Russell Lowell

Always operate on the basis that other people are basically warm, friendly, and sincere. Then treat them accordingly. Behavioral scientists have found that if you treat others in a certain way, they will tend to act that way toward you, even if they act

> Assume from the outset that another person is basically sincere, friendly, and well-meaning, regardless of the way he or she acts. This will be a correct assumption 80 percent of the time. (If you begin with the assumption that the other person is difficult to get along with, you will be correct almost 100 percent of the time.)

differently with other people. Paul R. Lawrence, associate professor of business administration at Harvard University, points out that many of us get into trouble because of our expectations that certain people are not pleasant or agreeable. We tend to prejudge. As a result, we often find people responding in the way we anticipated. It's the self-fulfilling prophecy.

The Art of Paraphrase

Paraphrasing another person's comments adds impact to your own communications. By acknowledging someone's opinion, taking it in, and repeating it, you reinforce and amplify it for the other person.

Paraphrasing can turn a heated argument into a constructive conversation. Marital counselors advise that couples can prevent spats from deteriorating into shouting sessions if they agree to follow one simple rule: When "A" has finished presenting a point, "B" must agree to rephrase that point, as he or she understands it, before making a new point. This way both partners show that they respect and, more important, understand the other's point of view.

When someone has expressed a negative feeling, the pendulum of his emotions is likely to swing just as far in the opposite direction *if he is not met head on with an argument.* Whenever you can, "concede before you contend" and paraphrase the other person's point or objection in the form of a question.

A good salesman always paraphrases a customer's opinion and feeds it back. The skilled automobile salesman says, "Now, Mrs. Jones, as I understand it, you like the roominess and comfort of this car, right?" This confirmation and amplification of the customer's statement could well be the turning point in the sale.

Empathy

We all possess a sixth sense about how others we know are reacting or feeling. This is sometimes called "social perception" or "empathy." Empathy seems to operate as a total feeling rather than as an impression formed on the basis of such obvious clues as posture, tone of voice, and facial expression. Often, our ability to empathize draws up on our knowledge of and past experience with the other person.

Dr. Carl Rogers has said, "The most powerful, persuasive force in interpersonal relations is the ability to perceive how another person feels—then to take on the other person's role in your imagination and reflect his own feelings back to him." In empathizing with other people, you sense how they feel and what their attitudes are. Then you put yourself in their "shoes" mentally and emotionally. This does not necessarily mean that you agree with them, but it does mean that you show appreciation and respect for their views. Once others perceive that you do have some "we" feeling for them and that you understand and respect their position, they are more likely to open up to other points of view.

It's All in How You Put It

One evening a young monk noticed one of the older monks smoking a pipe while reading his breviary. The young monk said, "Why, brother, I'm amazed to see you smoke while you pray! When I entered the monastery I asked the abbott if I could smoke while I prayed. He said, 'Of course not. I'm surprised you even asked!' "

"Well, now," said the old monk, "you didn't ask him right! You see, years ago I asked the reverend abbott the same question—but in a slightly different way. Am I correct in saying that you asked him 'Is it all right if I smoke while I pray?' "

"That's right," said the young monk.

"Well, brother," said the old monk with a twinkle in his eye, "I put it to him this way: 'Reverend Father, is it all right if I pray while I smoke?' 'Why, of course, my son,' said the abbott as he gave me his benediction. 'That's an excellent idea!' "

An aide to Lyndon Johnson once said this about the former President:

> *Many people have the mistaken idea that President Johnson rams his ideas down the throats of people by pure force. While Mr. Johnson can be forceful and do some positive selling when the occasion calls for it, he possesses, to a degree greater than I have ever seen in any other man, the ability to detect exactly what the other person's position is and why. Once he knows where the other person stands, he bones up on the other side of the argument and goes into the background and factors that led up to the other person's present position. Even when his own position is exactly opposite yours, he never once gives you the impression that he knows how you feel and why.*

Cultivating Friendships

An important factor in career success lies in cultivating new friendships and building contacts with key people. This is not to say that you should make friends just to use them. The only meaningful relationships are those that involve genuine concern, communication, and understanding. You can't fake it. You must get to know the other person's interests and needs. You must give the other person something of value, whether it's love, respect, or simply the fact that you have a valuable service to offer.

When you meet other people, project your best image. Be positive. Think big, talk big. If you tell others you're important, you will be.

Project a positive mental attitude in your conversations. Use vivid, cheerful words that convey a picture of enthusiasm, happiness, and success. Your enthusiasm is contagious and will be well received by everyone you meet.

Project self-confidence in the way you talk, listen, look, and react. Project your own feelings of worth and talk up the worth of others.

Project warmth and sincerity in all your communications. Greet others warmly with a firm handshake and direct eye-to-eye contact. Compliment others for a job well done. Have a good word for all.

> *When befriended, remember it; when you befriend, forget it.*
> —Benjamin Franklin

▪ Activity: Meet New People

1. Show genuine interest in a new acquaintance and listen attentively.
2. Talk a little about yourself, about items you've read in the newspaper or elsewhere. Use stories and anecdotes to make your points.
3. Make sure the person goes away knowing enough about you to remember you in the future and feels that you are interested in his or her activities. ▪

▪ Activity: Renew Old Friendships

1. On a piece of paper list your close friends and acquaintances. These are people on whom you might rely, even if you do not see them often.
2. Next to each name indicate how often you see the person. This can be a shocker, and you may be surprised at how many people you have neglected.
3. Send people you have neglected a postcard, pick up the phone and call, or write a note.
4. Preempt some prime television time to revive old friendships. Call someone for a round of golf or for an evening with you and your spouse. ▪

Review: Your Self-Image

Now that you've completed this section on the third checkpoint of potential, quickly score yourself by answering the following questions, using the scale at the bottom of the page.

1. Do you use your goal-oriented mind effectively? ___
2. Are you programming your mind to achieve your goals? ___
3. Does your self-image parallel your achievements? ___
4. Do you regard most work and social situations as opportunities rather than problems? ___
5. Do you accept yourself and your uniqueness? ___
6. Do you believe in yourself and your potential? ___
7. Are you actively building your self-image? ___
8. Do you know your strengths? ___
9. Do you reward yourself often for small successes? ___
10. Have you thought through your financial goals? ___
11. Do you have a healthy attitude toward money? ___
12. Do you "come across" well with people? ___

Scale

YES	10	Full use of potential
	9	Almost there
	8	Above average
	7	Average
	6	Below average
NO	5 4 3 2 1 0	Help!

Answer these questions about your responses to the questions above:

    Score 8–10   Am I satisfied?
                        Do I still want to improve?
                        How can I improve?
    Score 6–7   Is this acceptable to me?
                        Is it important to improve?
                        How can I improve?
    Score 5 or below What's happening? Why?
                        Is it important to improve?
                        How can I improve?

If you've identified any areas for improvement, answer the questions below:

    With whom can I discuss this problem?
    Who can give me counsel or direction in solving the problem?
    What step can I take *now* to do something to solve the problem?

Review Notes

Quickly review the marginal notes you have made and the exercises and activities you have done in this section. Summarize your thoughts below.

1. Ideas for follow-up developed as you read this section:

   _____
   _____
   _____
   _____
   _____

2. Ideas you believe should be included in your coordinated action plan:

   _____
   _____
   _____
   _____
   _____
   _____

3. Thoughts that occur to you at this time about
   (a) Using your self-image as a major tool for growth:

   (b) Your strengths and areas that need work:

   (c) Reinforcing your self-image through role playing and other techniques:

   (d) Money and your self-image:

4. Other thoughts:

Additional Reading

One action step available to help you improve is to learn more about an area suggested in this section. Here is a list of books you might consider for additional study:

Psycho-Cybernetics by Maxwell Maltz. Englewood Cliffs, N. J.: Prentice-Hall, 1960.

The Magic of Thinking Big by David J. Schwartz. New York: Cornerstone Library, 1965.

Think Rich by H. Stanley Judd. New York: Delacorte Press, 1978.

Your Erroneous Zones by Wayne Dyer. New York: Funk & Wagnalls, 1976.

Greatest Salesman in the World by Og Mandino. New York: Bantom Books, 1974.

Man's Search for Himself by Rollo May. New York: Dell Publishing Co., 1953.

SECTION V

Checkpoint 4: Your Productivity

The common idea that success spoils people by making them vain, egotistic, and self-complacent, is erroneous; on the contrary it makes them, for the most part, humble, tolerant, and kind. Failure makes people bitter and cruel.
—W. Somerset Maugham

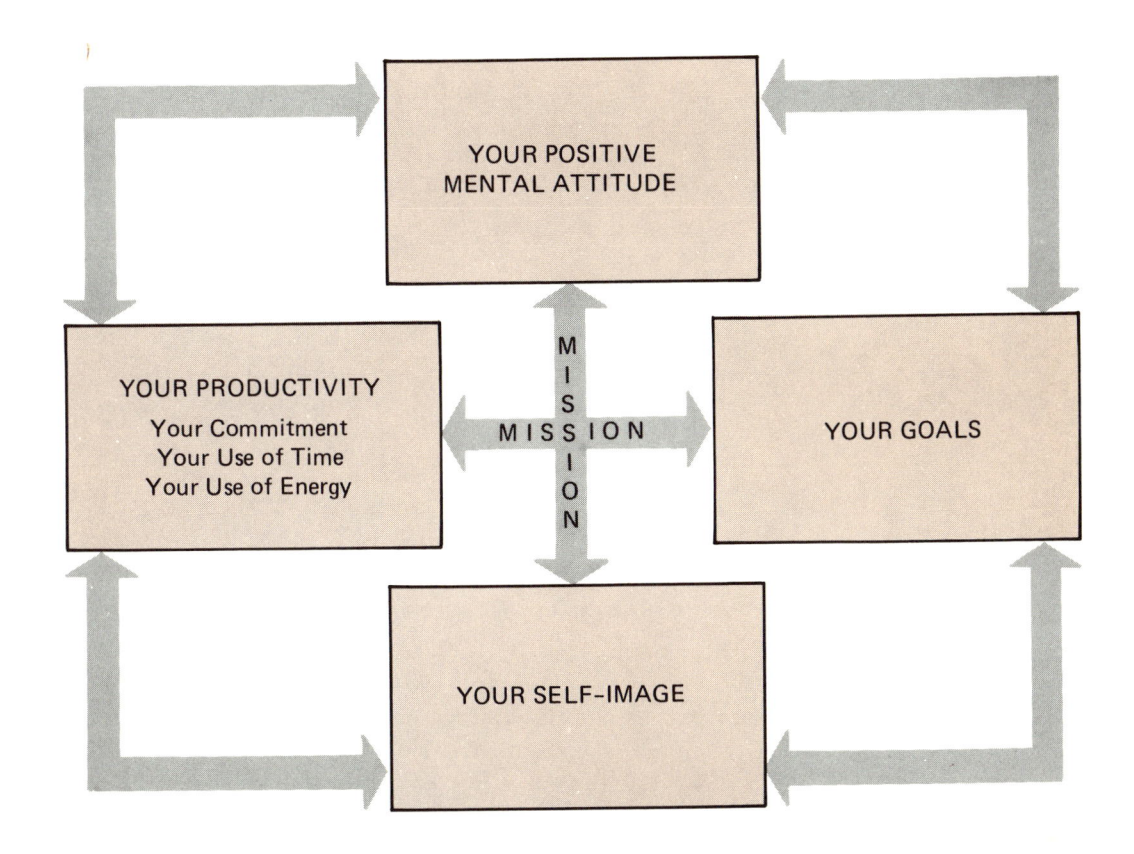

```
                    ┌──────────────────┐
                    │  YOUR POSITIVE   │
                    │ MENTAL ATTITUDE  │
                    └──────────────────┘
                             ↑
                             M
                             I
┌─────────────────┐          S          ┌──────────────┐
│ YOUR PRODUCTIVITY│ ← MISSION →        │  YOUR GOALS  │
│  Your Commitment │         I          │              │
│  Your Use of Time│         O          │              │
│  Your Use of Energy│       N          │              │
└─────────────────┘          ↓          └──────────────┘
                    ┌──────────────────┐
                    │  YOUR SELF-IMAGE │
                    └──────────────────┘
```

13. Your Commitment

All of us have a deep need to be actively involved in the world out there. We have a continuing need to build self-esteem, to be competent and productive, to be involved with others, and to feel that our lives count for something. In adulthood we may define ourselves chiefly in terms of external goals—job, family, or material advancement. At a later period in life we may become committed primarily to the betterment of our inner selves, or to making the world a better place.

Whatever our special purpose or plan, being fully involved means entering into a meaningful relationship with our commitments. It means setting action goals and action plans. A half-baked commitment leads to half-baked results.

Commitment generates the power, the motivation, the momentum to reach difficult goals. It isn't enough to decide to climb a mountain. Until you implement the decision, until you act, the decision is meaningless—it's a wish or an "I would like to" thought. Commitment means action, and ultimately you alone must generate the initiative to take the first step.

Here is what some well-known people have said about this commitment in getting to the top in their careers:

Inventor Howard Head, who made a fortune from the snow skis he designed, said that he succeeded because he continued to plug along despite repeated failures that would have defeated most people. Shortstop Larry Bowa said that his small size was a blessing in disguise because it forced him to try harder than everybody else. Heart surgeon Michael DeBakey claimed that he had single-minded commitment. General William Westmoreland said that he was dedicated to what he believed in.

In an interview in the *Philadelphia Inquirer* Dr. Harold Scheie, a noted ophthalmologist still in practice at age 71, talked about getting to the top:

I don't think I'm at the top, by any means, but in medicine, athletics, in anything, the people who get to the top are the people who are motivated. You look at some of the baseball players, and they're all in the right place at the right time. They are all fairly equal in ability, yet there's Pete Rose, who is in a class by himself. He's not great in anything but he goes all out all of the time.

In medicine, Scheie said, it works the same way:

Let me watch [young physicians] a week or two, and I'll tell you who will go to the top. He's the fellow who waits to see the last patient, who is the last to leave the hospital, who hates to leave the hospital. Maybe that's a definition of a workaholic, or maybe it's the definition of dedication. I don't know. But the people who are willing to go all out are the people who go all the way to the top.

It is fascinating to study the lives of those few individuals who reach the pinnacle of their careers. They make climbing to the top of some very high mountains look easy. Most people climb smaller peaks, but the principles and satisfactions can be the same. Here is what happens when you reach the top:

1. You go into "overdrive." You become a professional, performing your task effortlessly.
2. You use your imagination more. The roadblocks and tensions of the amateur are removed.
3. You become more excited and enthusiastic. You probably read and study or work more. Whatever it is you do, you do more of it and become better at it.
4. You enjoy your activity.

What Is Total Commitment?

After three lackluster years on Yale's track team, Frank Shorter, the 1972 Olympic Marathon winner, asked coach Bob Giegengack how he could become a good runner. Giegengack had a quick answer: "Give up skiing, drop the undergraduate glee club, eat the right foods, and get nine hours sleep a night." There, in one sentence, was the formula for changing an uncommitted amateur into a world-class athlete. Shorter followed his coach's advice, made a total commitment, and became a world champion.

It is difficult to overstate the rewards that occur as successful activity increases, as you adjust your thermostat to ever-increasing levels of productivity. Scientific studies show the effects of such activity: highly successful people enjoy markedly lower disability rates and longer life spans.

The Desire for Excellence

Pride of excellence is a primeval feeling, present even in animals. It is exhibited by the performing seal and by the setter bringing in its quarry. The desire for excellence is also instinctive. While people can live in reasonable happiness without fulfilling this need, life can be much richer and rewarding if you do something well. The degree to which you grow will depend on how much of yourself you bring to the task.

One of the major sources of distress in life is the lack of respect for one's own accomplishments. We tend to doubt the importance of our own achievements, especially as we grow older. There is no question that we all long for perfection. Nor is there any question that one of life's greatest satisfactions is to do our best and have it recognized, even if only by ourselves.

The other side of the coin is to avoid the humiliation and frustration of failure. Failure occurs when you consistently fall short of your attainable goals—when you know your performance is well below par. When you are fully committed to a goal, you automatically integrate your past experiences, education, training, and skills. You focus your entire being on a single objective. In so doing, you call forth your latent potential and creativity. You make it possible to achieve new levels of success. It is as if the act of commitment itself released resources you were unaware of.

> *Some people may have greatness thrust upon them. Very few have excellence thrust upon them.*
> —John Gardner

> You have a basic, instinctive desire to commit yourself to becoming what you want to become and to utilizing your potential to achieve your personal objectives. You have a built-in desire to excel within the range of your capabilities. If you don't recognize or fulfill this desire, you can pay a steep price in personal fulfillment—and in earnings.

Every company is aware of commitment when it hires a new employee. In one case, a new employee may do his job halfheartedly; he is there to do a day's work for a day's pay and little more. He is uninvolved and uncommitted. His job is merely a way of making a living. Another employee with the same job sees it as a challenge. She is fully involved in it and tries to find ways to make it more interesting and to do it better. Through her commitment, she begins to grow, begins to enlarge her self-concept. Her actions become apparent to superiors, and when the right job opens up, she is asked to accept it.

In business your effectiveness depends on your technical ability, management ability, intelligence, and personality. But what really sets you apart from the crowd is your commitment to your goals and to the work necessary to achieve them.

One individual looks at half a glass of water as half-empty; another looks at it as half-full. One person's dead-end job is another's steppingstone to achievement.

Mastering Your Career

We know that commitment and persistence in the pursuit of goals are primary requirements for success. Andrew Carnegie once explained his method: "Put all your eggs in one basket and keep your eye on the basket." Unless you are dedicated to your career, you can never become a master at it. In every field of endeavor, the price of success is the complete and undivided attention of the participant. You must be free of distractions and reasonably satisfied with your lot.

Here are the basic ingredients of commitment:

Hard Work.   Hard work is the key to self-mastery. There are no shortcuts. According to Ernest Newman, the English music critic, "Beethoven, Wagner, Bach, and Mozart settled down day

> A ruler gave his wise men a commission: "I want you to compile a book for me, *The Wisdom of the Ages,* that we may leave to posterity." After several years of work, the men returned to their ruler with twelve volumes. The ruler said, "I believe this is the wisdom of the ages, but it is so long I don't think people will read it. Condense it." Finally the wise men returned with only one book, but again it was too long. The wise men reduced the volume to a chapter, then a paragraph, and finally to a sentence.
>
> Their ruler was elated. "Gentlemen," he said, "this is truly the wisdom of the ages and as soon as people learn this truth, our problems will be solved."
>
> The sentence simply said, "There ain't no free lunch!"

after day to the job at hand with as much regularity as an accountant settles down each day to his figures. They did not waste time waiting for inspiration." If you aren't willing to work hard to master your career, to "pay the price," it just won't happen.

Discipline. You must discipline yourself to become a professional at your work—at whatever level you now find yourself. The great poet Robert Frost made a memorable comment when he said, "Life is tons of discipline." One of the mottos of the Olympics is "The essential thing is not winning, but fighting well." What discipline and control a Bruce Jenner and a Dorothy Hamill had to impose upon themselves to fight well and, in their case, to win.

Pablo Casals, at the height of his career, still practiced six hours every day. He was asked why the continued effort. His reply: "I think I'm making progress." Heavyweight champion James J. Corbett frequently said, "You become champion by fighting one more round. When things are tough, you fight one more round."

Talent. Hard work and discipline are no substitutes for talent. Many who try to master the piano with hard work and discipline finally give up in disgust. Yet these people are leaders in medicine, business, and other fields. If you don't have the talent for a particular task, it will be real drudgery. Matching your instinctive aptitudes and talents with the right career is perhaps the key to realizing your potential. Commitment comes easily when you enjoy what you're doing and do it well.

Building Your Commitment

It is human nature to make a commitment and then not stick to it. The classic case is the New Year's resolution to lose weight, stop smoking, exercise, or do better in your job. Sixty to ninety days later the resolve, the commitment, is long gone and forgotten. Many times the major reason for not following through is that you are not clear on the final destination. Here's how to strengthen your commitment and make it stick:

Define your goal in specific terms. Pick a major goal and use the procedure outlined in Chapter 17 to define it. This process helps you analyze important long-range goals and reduce them to manageable size.

Decide what you really want. Decide that you really want to achieve the goal you have listed. You must consciously *choose* success. You must decide to set a clear direction for yourself and to gain more control of your life.

Support your decision. Once you have mapped out your course and decided that you are willing to pay the price to achieve your goal, you need to gather information related to your objective. Get all the information you can from friends, experts, teachers, and psychologists, as well as from books, newspapers, magazines, seminars, and so on. If your goal is to get more exercise by swimming or playing tennis, look for books or magazines on the subject. Talk to your friends about it. How does it help them? Do they enjoy it? Does it give them more energy?

Examine your own thoughts and feelings. Are you withholding full commitment to your goals because of career indecision or because you can't take failure? You have to be honest with yourself, because you have to give at least 100 percent of yourself to be true to your goals. You'll find that difficult goals become easy if you make a total commitment.

Ralph Cordiner, former chairman of the board of General Electric Company, said this to a leadership conference: "We need from every man who aspires to leadership . . . a determination to undertake a personal program of self-development.

> Strong commitment and deep belief trigger you into finding ways to achieve your goals. When you know you can do it, the "how to" comes easily. When you make a big commitment and believe big, you grow big.

Nobody is going to order a man to develop. Whether a man lags behind or moves ahead in his specialty is a matter of his own personal application. This is something which takes time, work, and sacrifice. Nobody can do it for you."

> *What is the use of living, if it be not to strive for noble causes and to make this muddled world a better place to live in after we are gone?*
> —Winston Churchill

Whether you're in school, in the midst of a career, or approaching retirement, it is true that you will get out of life only what you put into it. I'm reminded of a story told during the 1972 presidential campaign. It seems a country gentleman wanted to board his horse. The first farmer he approached gave him a price of $25 a day, plus manure. The man thought this price too high and went to another farmer, who gave him a price of $15 plus the manure. On his third try he found a farmer who gave him a price of $5 a day to board the horse, with no mention of manure.

"But what about the manure?" the man asked.

The farmer replied, "For five dollars a day there won't be any."

■ Exercise: Building Commitment

1. Describe a goal and how you would achieve it.

_____
_____
_____
_____
_____

2. What information could you get together to help build your commitment?

_____
_____
_____
_____

3. What steps could you take right now to reach your goal?

_____
_____
_____
_____

4. What exercises and rewards could you use to reinforce your commitment?

_____
_____
_____
_____
_____

■

Put "Sizzle" in Your Goals

Visualize a steak sizzling on a charcoal grill. Think about it a moment. If you're like most people, you have just increased the probability that you will soon be dining on filet mignon.

In sales, you don't sell the steak you sell the sizzle. Similarly, in strategic planning, it's not the goal that keeps you on track but the "sizzle" of your goal. The more clearly you see your involvement with a project, an idea, or life itself, the more meaningful your commitment will be. If your goals sizzle for you, you are more likely to commit all your resources to them, with a far greater degree of growth and productivity.

Every one of your personal assets can be used to build commitment. You begin to develop sizzle when you identify goals that are significant to you and define them clearly; when you locate your strengths and the things you love doing; when you focus on key activities and use your time and energy effectively. Stress, your self-esteem, and your mental attitude all enter into the picture.

As you do the various exercises in this book, you will be creating your own "sizzle."

Practical Ways to Bolster Commitment

Write a brief résumé of your strengths and past history as if you were applying for your lifetime job. Assess your potential for growth. Give it your best shot and read your résumé every month or two.

Read books and listen to tapes that inspire you toward a particular goal. Frequent repetition is important to sustain commitment. Use your own notes in these pages as a permanent reference for reinforcing your commitment.

Each day rehearse your goals. Visualize in your mind the successful achievement of your goal. Successful athletes—swimmers, golfers, track stars—"psych themselves up" before the event. Just as the professional golfer makes a dry run of the course—the traps, the water hazards, and the distances—before the tournament, so you can mentally prepare the course you will follow toward your goal. Be alert for trouble spots, but make sure your attitude is positive. After all, the way in which you think about yourself often becomes a self-fulfilling prophecy. Forecast your own success.

Take the first step. Once you take the first step toward a goal, your chances of being successful zoom. In order to develop your commitment, start with small steps. For example, if your goal is to improve your time management skills, rather than spend a lot of money at first on an expensive timekeeping machine, begin by looking through a catalog of office products. Or buy a book to record a "to do" list or a basket for your desk to help organize your tasks. If the change is a major one such as a new career, you may want to try out the career on a part-time or freelance basis first to find out if it is suitable.

Stimulate your interest with something related to your goal. If your goal is to spend more time pleasurably at work, you might rearrange the working space, buy an attractive plant for the room, or purchase a new calendar or appointment book. If your goal is to take up jogging, you might stimulate your interest by buying a book on the subject or new jogging shoes. Motivating yourself takes some imagination, but why not make the task a little more enjoyable as you reinforce your commitment?

> *Luck is a crossroad where preparation and opportunity meet.*
> —*Anonymous*

14. Your Use of Time

Each of us has exactly the same amount of time each day. The key to improving productivity is not how much time we have, but how well we use the time available.

Time is a resource which all of us must spend at the rate of 60 seconds a minute. We cannot stockpile it and we cannot save it; but we can manage it. Peter Drucker has said, "Time is the scarcest resource and unless it is managed, nothing else can be managed."

The efficient use of time is a critical element in adjusting the level of our activity. Yet this vital resource is often misunderstood, mismanaged, and in large part left to chance. How can we learn to treat this priceless asset less casually? The answer lies not in managing the clock better, but in managing ourselves better with respect to the clock.

Habits and Time

Many activities in daily life are repeated so often that we do them virtually out of habit. We dress, eat, drive, and do a thousand routine tasks without much conscious thought. William James said, "We must make automatic and habitual as early as possible as many useful actions as we can. . . . The more details of our daily life we can hand over to the effortless custody of automatism, the more our higher powers of mind will be set free for the proper work."

James stated three keys to the acquisition of habits:

1. Launch the new practice as strongly as possible.
2. Never let an exception occur until the new habit is firmly rooted.
3. Seize the first possible chance to act on your resolution.

As James put it, "A tendency to act becomes effectively ingrained in proportion to the frequency with which the actions actually occur." Don't procrastinate!

Just as important as developing new habits is overcoming bad ones. Benjamin Franklin once wrote that it was essential for people to note their behavior and then develop a system to eliminate undesirable habits. He said: "I concluded, at length, that the mere speculative conviction that it was in our interest to be completely virtuous was not sufficient to prevent our slipping; and that contrary habits must be broken, and good ones acquired and established, before we can have any dependence on a steady, uniform rectitude of conduct."

Franklin's method was twofold:

1. To define the desirable behaviors he wanted to achieve, including temperance, silence, order, resolution, sincerity, justice, moderation, cleanliness, tranquility, and humility.
2. To select one behavior each week to work on, using a weekly calendar to track his progress.

	Sun.	Mon.	Tues.	Wed.	Thurs.	Fri.	Sat.
Temperance Eat not to dullness Drink not to elevation						X	

From the above chart we see that Franklin achieved his objective until Friday, when he judged he had overindulged. By using this method he was able to change some of his bad habits.

Time Traps

Effective time management increases your awareness of and response to the present moment. It means that you are functioning effectively in the here and now. Just as important as scheduling time is knowing the various time traps that can ensnare the most sophisticated and complicate greatly the climb to the top of the mountain. By being aware of these traps and avoiding them, you can revitalize the goal-setting process and

> *Every single qualification for success is acquired through habit:* If you do not deliberately form good habits, then unconsciously you will form bad ones. You are the kind of person you are because you have formed the habit of being that kind of person, and the only way you can change is through habit.

gain time for new projects and activities. You become the master instead of the servant of time.

The Preoccupation Trap. Although habits are generally indispensable, they can also impare the effective use of your time. As long as the task is routine and the circumstances basically unchanging, you can go on automatic pilot, with your thoughts elsewhere—on planning, speculating, or daydreaming. But if the situation is fluid and there are alternatives to be considered, you can't be lost in thought if you are to avoid disaster.

"Tuning out" when others are talking, daydreaming, and absentmindedness are but a few of the symptoms of preoccupation. If you observe other people you will see these habits in abundance. Lack of alertness doesn't solve problems; it causes them.

- When you are preoccupied you may miss a vital part of what your boss or customer is telling you.
- Because of inattention you may speak out of turn and destroy an important relationship.
- If you are preoccupied, you may not be able to see that your listener is confused and does not clearly understand what you are saying.

In essence whenever you are preoccupied or inattentive, you have lost the freedom to manage your time. Lack of alertness, or preoccupation, is a vital factor in reducing career output and promotability. If you increase the number of moments during the day when you are alert and giving full attention to what is going on, you will be more productive and more successful.

The Activity Trap. A basic principle of time management is to work on activities that lead you toward your goals. You fall into the activity trap when *being busy* becomes a substitute for *meeting your goals.* Your emphasis is on "clock time" rather than on "goal time." Carrying on activities long after they have served their purpose is the most common cause of the mismanagement of time.

> *One of the best ways of avoiding necessary and even urgent tasks is to seem to be busily employed on things that are already done.*
> —John Kenneth Galbraith

There is a normal tendency to become so enmeshed in the activities leading to a goal that the activities become ends in themselves. For example, more often than not the life insurance salesman falls into the activity trap. As he starts his career of selling he sets production goals, and over the first three years he establishes himself in the business. At the same time, he engages in clusters of activities that contribute to his success. But invariably as he realizes a certain degree of success, these activities become set in concrete:

- If he has been spending more time in the office than he should—he stays that way.
- If he does far more paperwork than he should—he continues that way indefinitely.
- If he is wasting valuable time talking with associates—the habit continues ad infinitum. In general his activities have become routine, boring, and definitely nonproductive.

When goals become centered on activities rather than on results, you begin to lose enthusiasm—you get into a rut. Boredom sets in and what a disaster! Your commitment weakens. Your use of time becomes increasingly inefficient. Finally, your self-image narrows and you perform at a low, often stressful level.

The solution? Obviously, if you are caught in the activity trap, you must first become aware of it. You can correct the problem by restructuring your goals to get yourself back on course. Then you must never lose sight of your goals, short and long term. Easy? No. Worthwhile? You bet your life!

The 80/20 Trap. The Pareto principle, named after the nineteenth-century Italian economist, states that the majority of people spend about 80 percent of their time on activities that produce approximately 20 percent of their results. The chart below illustrates this principle.

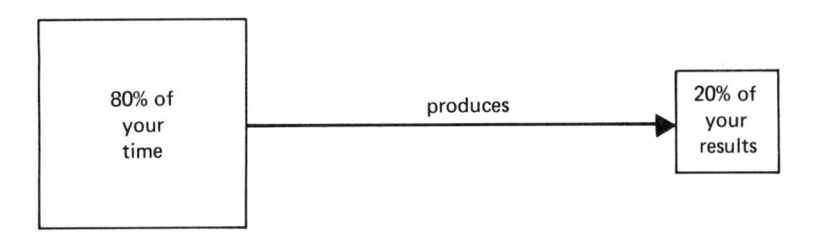

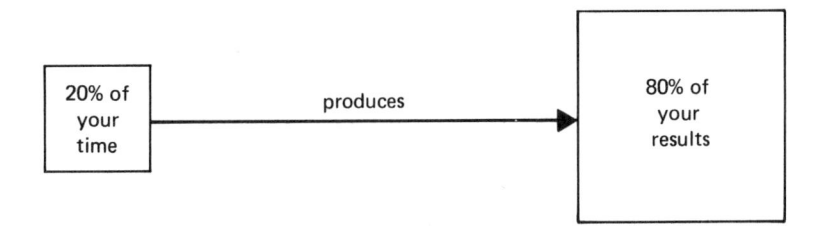

```
┌─────────┐                          ┌─────────┐
│ 80% of  │                          │ 20% of  │
│  your   │ ──── produces ────▶      │  your   │
│  time   │                          │ results │
└─────────┘                          └─────────┘


┌───────┐                              ┌─────────┐
│20% of │                              │ 80% of  │
│ your  │ ──── produces ────▶          │  your   │
│ time  │                              │ results │
└───────┘                              └─────────┘
```

Here are a few examples of the 80/20 rule:

- Analysis shows that out of an eight-hour day a salesman spends less than two hours actually selling.
- After a study of its sales accounts by size, an insurance company found that less than 10 percent of its accounts comprised 90 percent of its sales volume. By concentrating its efforts on this small group of accounts, it achieved substantial sales and profit gains the following year.
- A university study revealed that only a 5 percent increase in effort was needed to raise a student's mark by one full grade.

Avoiding Time Traps. How can you work around time traps? Be aware of them! Then when you find yourself preoccupied, daydreaming, or turning on the TV out of habit, simply say, "Hey, I don't want to do this now." Remember that you have the power, at any time, to change your actions and in so doing to change the quality of your life.

Use the principle of coordination of assets. Don't condemn or criticize yourself if you have poor time habits—most people do. Get excited about what a change might mean. Picture in your mind what the change would be like. Then:

1. *Prepare a coordinated goals statement.* (See Chapter 17.) Break your goals down into those with high value, medium value, and low value. Define subgoals and the activities needed to achieve them, and set priorities for your activities.

2. *Prepare a "to do" list.* Establish your daily priorities, delegate responsibilities, and schedule your plans.

3. *Keep a daily record of your activities.* Check on where your time goes and review your progress in achieving your goals.

4. *Keep asking the question "What is the best use of my time right now?"*

> *He slept beneath the moon*
> *He basked beneath the sun*
> *He lived a life of going-to-do*
> *And died with nothing done.*
> —James Albery

■ Exercise: Increasing Your Productive Time

Write down how you might improve your results if you were to increase your most productive time to 30 or 40 percent or more of your day.

_____
_____
_____
_____
_____

The Time Log

To begin managing your time better, keep a daily time log to find out where your time is really going. Review it at the end of each week. You'll be amazed at how much of your time is actually wasted. You will probably find that you waste time pretty much the same way every day. This should give you the motivation you need to begin to manage yourself and your time more effectively.

Record your activities in the time log for four weeks. At the end of each week, identify ten major activities that waste your time. For example:

    Telephone interruptions
    Drop-in visitors
    Leaving tasks unfinished
    Not listening
    Lack of objectives
    Unclear instructions
    Incorrect dictation
    Coffee breaks
    Mistakes
    Trying to do too much

Daily Time Log

Time	Task To Be Done	*Priority* 1. Urgent 2. Important 3. Not vital 4. Routine	*Priority* Eliminate Delegate Consolidate Other
8:00			
8:30			
9:00			
9:30			
10:00			
10:30			
11:00			
11:30			
2:00			
2:30			
3:00			
3:30			
4:00			
4:30			
5:00			
5:30			
Evening			

After four weeks, establish a permanent program to eliminate those timewasters that periodically appear. Then embark on a program for constructively using the time you are now wasting.

■ Exercise: Identifying Timewasters

As you look back each week at your time log, identify your top timewasters in order of importance. Identify your secretary's top timewasters as well.

My Top Timewasters	My Secretary's Top Timewasters
1. _____	1. _____
2. _____	2. _____
3. _____	3. _____
4. _____	4. _____
5. _____	5. _____
6. _____	6. _____
7. _____	7. _____
8. _____	8. _____
9. _____	9. _____
10. _____	10. _____

■

Making Better Use of Your Time

Scheduling your time is fundamental to your growth and to realizing your potential. Here are some key points to remember:

Big events demand big time. Allow ample time for the important events on your schedule each day. No task should be handled in an atmosphere of haste. It is important not to clutter your mind or to be led into a state of panic by trying to catch up.

Eliminate or delegate. Eliminate those items from your calendar that are not economically worth your time—or delegate them. If you are doing a job worth $4 an hour when you are being paid $10, $15, or $20 an hour, you are obviously squandering your time—and potential. There is great value in costing out your activities. Delegate, delegate, delegate!

Allow no interruptions. Don't permit yourself to be interrupted frequently during an assigned task. Starting and stopping a job in order to answer questions, talk on the phone, or embark on some other project can sap your energy, destroy your concentration, and diminish your effectiveness. If necessary, go off somewhere and hide until you've completed your project—and don't tell anybody where you've gone!

Do one job at a time. Focus your efforts on one job at a time in the order listed on your daily schedule. Finish what you start. Jumping from job to job destroys your momentum and requires additional energy to "crank yourself up" for each new task. Wheelspinning has killed more people on the job than on the highway.

Simplify. Simplify complicated jobs and goals. Breaking a big job down into components makes it easier to accomplish and helps you use your time more effectively. For example, a yearly objective that seems insurmountable may be quite simple if it is approached on a daily basis.

Eric Sevareid, the well-known television commentator, said, "Years ago I took on a daily writing and broadcasting chore that now has totaled 2,000 scripts. Had I been asked to sign a contract to write 2,000 scripts, I would have refused in despair. But I was asked only to write one—the next one—and that is all I have ever done."

Concentrate. The ability to concentrate on and complete a task enables those of modest talent to reach heights of achievement that can elude even the very talented. A good exam-

> Charles Schwab, the former president of Bethlehem Steel and one of the few men ever paid $1 million a year, was fretting because he couldn't seem to get enough done. Details and minor matters kept crowding in on his time, keeping him from getting to more important tasks. He asked a management consultant what to do about it. The consultant handed Schwab a blank sheet of paper and said, "Write down the six most important things you intend to do tomorrow. Tomorrow morning start on the first item and work on it until it's finished. Then go on to the next item." Schwab tried the idea and found it so helpful that he recommended it to his associates and, reportedly, sent the consultant a check for $25,000 in appreciation.

ple of the value of concentration is Harry Hopkins, President Roosevelt's confidential adviser in World War II. Physically disabled in later life, Hopkins could work only a few hours a day. He was forced to cut out all but the most vital matters, but he did not become ineffective. Rather he became, as Churchill called him once, "Lord Heart of the Matter" and accomplished more than anyone else in wartime Washington. Physical necessity forced Hopkins to focus his time in a brilliantly effective way.

Do it now. Make it a practice to take an action, make a decision, dispose of a letter, or whatever *the first chance you get*. Unless you have good reason to defer action, you should develop this vital habit of self-management. The do-it-now person is in the minority, and nailing down this habit takes practice, discipline, and an iron will.

■ *Activity: Do It Now!*

1. Select a task, sit down, and get started.
2. Think for short periods of time and reward yourself frequently.
3. Eliminate the anxiety of having to do something by making the event happen right now.

> *I never did anything worth doing by accident; nor did any of my inventions come by accident. They came by work.*
> —Thomas Edison

Practical Tips on Using Time

Here are a few quick ideas to help you manage your time more effectively:

1. Skim books quickly when looking for ideas.
2. Give up "waiting" time—consider it a time to relax, plan, or do something for fun.
3. Jot down notes or ideas. Keep a pad and pencil handy.
4. Review your goals once a month. Keep signs in the office or at home reminding you of what the goals are. Plan and set priorities.

5. Schedule activities months in advance to give your life variety and balance and to free your time. Reward yourself when things are accomplished.
6. Work smarter rather than harder.
7. Focus on top-priority jobs.
8. Give yourself enough time to concentrate on high-priority items.
9. Do much of your thinking on paper.
10. Set deadlines.
11. Learn to listen.
12. Learn to delegate.
13. Make use of specialists.

15. Your Use of Energy

All those who achieve mastery over themselves consider storing their energy as fundamental. Assuming you are in good health, successful activity (both physical and mental) is the best way to conserve your energy.

But, you say, doesn't successful activity *consume* energy? The truth is successful activity, no matter how intense, creates joy, satisfaction, *and* energy. Failure, in the guise of self-criticism, defensiveness, boredom, or worry, creates energy leaks that breed fatigue and that suck up energy at an incredible rate. As Vince Lombardi, the late-great Green Bay Packer coach, put it, "Fatigue makes cowards of us all."

■ Activity: Put Negatives to Work

Take your negative feelings (depression, anger, frustration) and put them to work for you. Instead of fighting them, ask yourself:

"What can I learn from this?"
"What can I do that is more positive?"
"How can I treat myself better?"

Then turn your energy loss to useful purpose. ■

Energy and Your Emotions

Eric Taylor, author of *Fitness After Forty*, says enthusiasm is the real answer to feeling better and gaining energy. "Your mind governs the way you feel," he notes, "and the vigor of your emotions can revitalize your muscles." But, he adds, you have to get the proper rest and exercise as well as eat the right foods. Taylor cites evidence that enthusiasm and excitement stimulate the adrenal glands, which pump hormones into the bloodstream to help the liver release energy fuel.

Set a goal today of feeling better and more energetic. Get enough sleep, eat moderately, cut down alcoholic drinks—be positive and upbeat and you'll find new life. Start with gentle exercise. Move around in the evening. Go outdoors for a breath of fresh air, go for a walk or jog. Do anything, but don't surrender to fatigue.

Fatigue is often emotional in origin and is frequently related to boredom. If you suffer from extreme boredom, you are likely to start the morning tired and have little energy during the day. More rest isn't the answer. Somehow you must renew the challenge—find new interest in your career or find outlets outside of your career. Or perhaps change your career. A comprehensive evaluation of the checkpoints of potential in this book can help you come to grips with the problem of emotional fatigue.

Energy and Negativism

Self-criticism can be a real energy-stealer. All of us tend to condemn ourselves unnecessarily. We take an action, using our best judgment. Then a day or a week later, with our infallible 20/20 hindsight, we criticize our decision.

■ *Activity: Conserve Your Energy*

1. Split the day into small segments of time. Treat each segment as important in itself. Develop a sense of achievement out of each segment. Focus your energy.
2. Complete every action. Start with a simple problem and move up. Energy flows like electricity and must not be interrupted.
3. Develop the energy look. Move decisively, stand erect, hold your head up.
4. Reward yourself frequently as you complete small tasks. ■

> Rather than brood over a mistake, ask yourself: "What can I do right now that will help the most?" Once you find the answer, stop further questioning and act. And no post-mortems!

Energy and Nutrition

"You are what you eat," as the saying goes. The relationship between your diet and your mental and physical well-being is well documented. Yet the medical profession continues to put nutrition on the back burner in considering the "whole" patient. Most specific diseases can be treated with drugs and surgical procedures. But achieving "wellness," or peace of mind, is another story. For one thing, if nutrition is neglected, it can dramatically affect your energy, emotions, potential, and, in the long run, your health.

Dr. William Lederer, a psychiatrist and co-author of the classic novel *The Ugly American*, has found that low sugar tolerance, food allergies, and low levels of trace metals or vitamins exercise a marked influence on behavior. He points out that as blood sugar drops, people often start behaving erratically.

Dr. Lederer, who is currently researching problem marriages, notes in a recent newspaper interview that nutrition can play a role in marital disharmony: "We've learned that 57 percent of discordant married couples are in biochemical imbalance—some form of malnutrition—and their behavior becomes unpredictable. You can have all the blasted psychological treatment you want, from Sigmund Freud or anybody, and if you've got nutrition problems the negative behavior still comes popping out."

A 1977 U.S. Senate report noted that most Americans have poor dietary habits.* The average American eats too much red meat, salt, and sugar and not enough fruits, grains, and vegetables. The report recommended these dietary goals for U.S. families:

1. Increase your carbohydrate consumption to account for 55 to 60 percent of your energy (caloric intake).
2. Reduce your overall fat consumption from approximately 40 to 30 percent of your energy intake.
3. Reduce your saturated fat consumption to account for about 10 percent of your total energy intake and balance that with poly-unsaturated and mono-unsaturated fats, each of which should account for about 10 percent of your energy intake.

Dietary Goals for the United States, prepared by the Select Committee on Nutrition and Human Needs of the United States Senate, February 1977.

4. Reduce your cholesterol consumption to about 300 milligrams a day.
5. Reduce your sugar consumption by about 40 percent, to account for about 15 percent of your total energy intake.
6. Reduce your salt consumption by about 50 to 85 percent, to approximately 3 grams a day.

Energy and Physical Fitness

Four hundred years ago, Montaigne wrote: "Health is a precious thing . . . the only thing that deserves to be pursued at the expense not only of time, sweat, labor, worldly goods, but of life itself; since without health, pleasures, wisdom, knowledge, lose their color and fade away. To my mind, no way that leads to health can be rugged, no means dearly bought."

A physical-conditioning program can produce marked changes in your mental outlook and energy level. Good posture, a trim physique, added confidence, a feeling of aliveness, and an increased enjoyment of life—all can be benefits of physical conditioning. The idea that a person older than 40 is "over the hill"

has changed. The pot belly and waning sexual and physical powers are not inevitable. Doctors have found that the decline in physical and mental ability occurs primarily because of lack of exercise. There is no biological imperative that people are ready for the scrap heap at 55 or 60. Your body is like a fine piece of machinery—it will function well as long as you treat it well.

> *It is tragic when a man outlives his body.*
> —Sigmund Freud

Here are some physical-conditioning ideas for the busy person.

Start the day with a brisk walk. Even a few minutes of walking can do wonders. Renew your vigor by breathing deeply.

Relax several times during the day. Use the relaxation technique for two to three minutes.

After working hours, continue with physical activities. Try jogging, golf, tennis, swimming, or any other sport that takes you outdoors. You need cardiovascular conditioning as well as recreational activity.

When you are tired, get up from your chair and stretch. This exercise can be done at any time and will get the kinks out. Breathe slowly and deeply. In Yoga, breathing is called "prana," the life force.

Take frequent breaks and vacations from your routine. It's important to your health and well-being that you separate yourself from your work periodically.

Eat sparingly. Avoid large meals, particularly at lunch. Eat nutritious food.

Exercise and the Quality of Life

At a three-day conference on the role of exercise in preventing physical decline (held in October 1977 at the National Institutes of Health in Maryland), these points of agreement emerged:

1. Walking is the most efficient form of exercise.
2. Exercise has a protective effect during stress.

3. Exercised bones are far less likely to break or lose their range of motion.
4. Exercised cardiovascular systems and lungs show a marked improvement in functioning.
5. Exercise has striking benefits in preventing obesity.
6. Exercise improves the quality of life.

The results of this conference confirm the vital need to coordinate your assets—mental, physical, and emotional. Note especially point 6: that reasonable exercise "improves the quality of life." It has been said that the key to fulfillment lies not in adding more years to your life, but in adding more life to your years. It's exciting to contemplate how a good exercise program can enhance not only your lifestyle and response to stress but all the checkpoints of potential.

Because regular exercise demands a sharply defined regimen and a fixed time schedule, it is ideal for structuring goals. A regular commitment to exercise—whether jogging, tennis, gymnastics, or swimming—gives you a structure to work with. The sense of confidence and pride you derive from becoming fit shows in every action. You not only look good but, more important, you feel good. Exercise gives you a psychological high that can carry over into your other activities.

The physical self communicates the inner self to the world. Your body expresses a great deal about who you feel you are.

Review: Your Productivity

Now that you've completed this section on the fourth checkpoint of potential, quickly score yourself by answering the following questions using the scale at the bottom of the page.

1. Do you know what you really want? ___
2. Are you fully committed to achieving it? ___
3. Are you enjoying what you are doing? ___
4. Are you willing to "pay the price"? ___
5. Do you write down your goals, plans, and ideas? ___
6. Do you use your time effectively? ___
7. Do you act on things without delay? ___
8. Can you focus on the present moment without becoming preoccupied by other thoughts? ___
9. Are you a victim of the activity trap? ___
10. Are you a victim of the 80/20 trap? ___
11. Do you conserve your energy for important tasks? ___
12. Are your nutritional habits good? ___
13. Do you have a satisfactory exercise program? ___

Scale

	10	Full use of potential
YES	9	Almost there
	8	Above average
	7	Average
	6	Below average
	5	
NO	4	
	3	Help!
	2	
	1	
	0	

Answer these questions about your responses to the questions above:

  Score 8–10 Am I satisfied?
         Do I still want to improve?
         How can I improve?
  Score 6–7   Is this acceptable to me?
         Is it important to improve?
         How can I improve?
  Score 5 or below What's happening? Why?
         Is it important to improve?
         How can I improve?

If you've identified any areas for improvement, answer the questions below:

  With whom can I discuss this problem?
  Who can give me counsel or direction in solving the problem?
  What step can I take *now* to do something to solve the problem?

Review Notes

Quickly review the marginal notes you have made and the exercises and other activities you have done in this section. Summarize your thoughts below:

1. Ideas for follow-up developed as you read this section:

_____
_____
_____
_____

2. Ideas you believe should be included in your coordinated action plan:

_____
_____
_____
_____

3. Thoughts that occur to you at this time about
   (a) Having a meaningful and satisfying commitment to your goals:

   _____
   _____
   _____
   _____
   _____

   (b) Your productivity in general:

   _____
   _____
   _____
   _____
   _____

   (c) Your use of time:

   _____
   _____
   _____
   _____
   _____

   (d) Your energy level:

   _____
   _____
   _____
   _____
   _____

4. Other thoughts:

   _____
   _____
   _____
   _____
   _____

Additional Reading

One action step available to help you improve is to learn more about an area suggested in this section. Here is a list of books you might consider for additional study:

The Time Trap by R. Alec MacKenzie. New York: AMACOM, 1972.

Management of Time by James T. McCay. Englewood Cliffs, N. J.: Prentice-Hall, 1959.

How to Get Control of Your Time and Your Life by Alan Lakein. New York: Signet Books, 1973.

Getting Organized by Stephanie Winston. New York: Warner Books, 1978.

Excellence by John W. Gardner. New York: Harper & Row, 1961.

Towards a Psychology of Being by Abraham H. Maslow. New York: D. Van Nostrand Company, 1968.

SECTION VI

Strategic Life Planning

Wisdom is the ability to see the long-run consequences of current actions, the willingness to sacrifice short-run gains for larger long-run benefits, and the ability to control that which is controllable and not to fret over what is not. Therefore, the essence of wisdom is concern with the future. It is not the type of concern with the future that the fortune teller has; he only tries to predict it. The wise man tries to control it. . . . Planning is the design of a desired future and of effective ways of bringing it about.

—Russell L. Ackoff
A Concept of Corporate Planning

16. Building Your Life Strategy

As our world has become more complex, the need to develop and coordinate our personal plans has become more urgent. Many major and costly mistakes can be avoided through strategic planning. Our educational system is not equipped to prepare us for the broad-range planning necessary to survive happily in today's world. If we are lucky we have a wise parent, a mentor, or a manager who has the vision to show us the larger picture of life and to inspire us at an early age. But few of us learn to use the world instead of being used by it. It is far easier to be a "reactor" rather than an "actor" in life. When we don't climb our mountain we may give up, give in, or surrender ourselves to others as the price of our survival.

Our rules for living are formed by our family, our profession, our religion, and anything else that provides us with guidelines. The problem is not in the guidelines themselves, which are important, but in their potential to obscure the fact that we have a life apart from our job, our family, and other people. I knew a widow, a dear person, who told me after her husband died, "I don't want to live; he was my life." She died within the year, as if she had willed herself into the grave.

The objective of strategic planning is to regain a beachhead on our independence and to assume control over that which is controllable. Such a process helps us clarify our goals and thus regain the sense of mission so essential to vigorous, effective living.

The Nature of Coordinated Planning

Most people lose some of the joy of life as they get older. This focuses attention on several questions being asked by people today: "How can I recapture the joy of life that began when I was born?" "How can I make my life more meaningful?" "How can I climb my own mountain?" While there is no simple answer to these questions, the place to start is certainly with personal planning.

In military operations, the leaders take into consideration their mission, the resources and alternatives available to accomplish that mission, the conflicts they are likely to encounter, and the coordination they must effect between various groups in order to succeed. All these factors are considered before the final operational plan is drawn up.

The approach is much the same in strategic life planning. By studying where you want to go (your life mission), what resources you have to get there (your goals, skills, financial means, and so on), the various ways of getting there, the potential obstacles, and how you must coordinate your goals with other people (your spouse, for instance), you arrive at your coordinated life plan. This plan becomes your personal blueprint for fulfillment, and like a military battle plan, its success or failure is often determined on the drawing board.

Most of us start life planning only in times of crisis. The loss of a job, illness, the death of a spouse, retirement—these are some of the reasons we seek help. It is particularly at such times that we must maintain a positive mental attitude, focus on new and challenging goals, and devise workable plans to keep us growing. Otherwise we will be unprepared for either adversity or opportunity. Think about it for a moment:

- Even though you're terribly busy, can you afford to leave major aspects of your life to chance?
- Isn't it better to put in some hard thinking now to prepare for the difficult life adjustments you may need to make later?
- Because life is a gamble, isn't it logical to define what you want, to organize yourself so that you are prepared to take advantage of whatever comes your way? It's a question of "stacking the odds in your favor."

You can improve your self-image and effectiveness 100 percent if you think of yourself as an active agent in molding your life. Coordinated planning is a key element in realizing your potential. It shapes your life by giving you (1) specific goals and priorities, (2) a balance among the working, learning, and leisure aspects of your life, and (3) new horizons.

Remember as you develop your life plan that there is *no one plan, no one right way.* This book presents a smorgasbord of approaches and philosophies. Your job is to identify those ideas that are pertinent to your situation and to tailor a program that will help you realize your potential. Once you understand the life planning process, you will be able to apply it over and over again throughout your life. Circumstances may change, but the process remains the same.

The Stages of Life

Traditional wisdom holds that life consists of three separate and distinct stages:

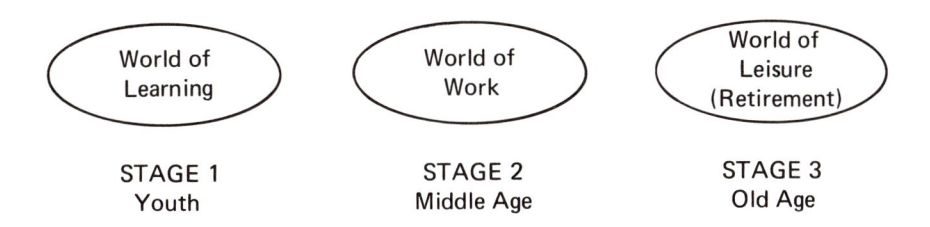

```
   World of            World of           World of
   Learning             Work              Leisure
                                        (Retirement)

   STAGE 1             STAGE 2            STAGE 3
    Youth             Middle Age          Old Age
```

In his book *The Three Boxes of Life*, Richard Bolles points out that these three worlds—education, work, and leisure—have become so isolated from each other that most people feel they have little preparation for each stage. For example, many of those entering the working world feel that they are poorly prepared for finding a job. And those about to retire feel that they have had little preparation for a life of leisure.

> *Most of us progressively narrow the scope and variety of our lives. . . . Reject stagnation. Reject the myth that learning is for young people.*
> —John Gardner

Highly successful people blend these three worlds throughout their lives so that at any given stage they are learning, working, and playing simultaneously. For these fortunate people, work is a form of play as well as a learning process. This is the type of situation all of us should be in.

Using coordinated planning, we *can* put all three worlds in balance throughout our lives, so that our "circles of life" would look like this:

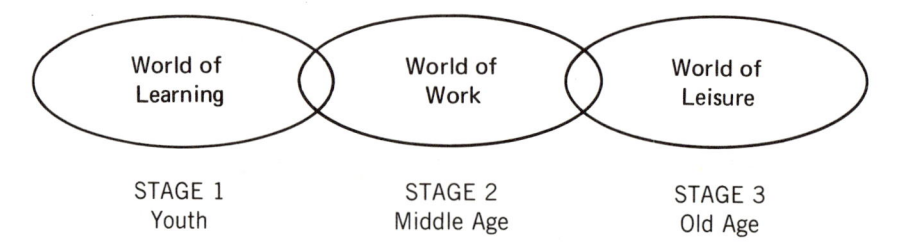

```
   World of       World of       World of
   Learning        Work          Leisure

   STAGE 1        STAGE 2        STAGE 3
   Youth          Middle Age     Old Age
```

As you construct your life plan in this and the following chapter, try to include goals for the learning, working, and leisure phases of your life. For each phase, ask yourself:

"Am I satisfied with where I am now?"
"If not, where would I like to be?"
"What do I have to do to get there?"

Project your thoughts. Dream. What would you like to have accomplished by this time next year? Three years from now? Ten? Let your plans encompass family, career, health, and all your other assets. Remember—goals start with hopes and dreams.

Reviewing Your Mission and Goals

The earlier sections in this book were designed to help you begin developing your coordinated life plan. Before you continue, review the personal mission statement you prepared in Chapter 3. Does this statement still reflect the central theme of your life?

Does it portray what you are all about? (If you are satisfied with the statement, fine. If not, take the time now to revise it so that it accurately portrays your thinking at this time.)

In the same way, review the goals statements you worked on at the end of Chapter 8. Are any changes indicated at this time?

Have any additional items occurred to you? If so, revise your goals lists to reflect your current feelings.

You are now ready to embark on the final four steps of the life planning process:

1. Evaluating the checkpoints of potential.
2. Summarizing your goals.
3. Setting your priorities.
4. Coordinating your priorities.

Step One: Evaluating the Checkpoints of Potential

As you reviewed the four checkpoints of potential earlier in this book, you made notes, completed exercises, and summarized certain facts about yourself at the end of each section. However, at that time, each section more or less stood by itself. Coordinated personal planning requires that the observations you made and the scoring exercises you completed be brought together to focus on the key aspects of your final plan. On the following pages review the notes you made at the end of each checkpoint section.

**Checkpoint 1: Your Positive Mental Attitude
(Section II, Chapters 3, 4, 5)**

List below those ideas you identified for specific attention in your coordinated life plan. Add others that may have occurred to you since.

_____
_____
_____
_____
_____
_____
_____
_____
_____
_____
_____

**Checkpoint 2: Your Goals
(Section III, Chapters 6, 7, 8)**

List below those ideas you identified for specific attention in your coordinated life plan. Add others that may have occurred to you since.

_____
_____
_____
_____
_____
_____
_____
_____
_____
_____
_____

Checkpoint 3: Your Self-Image
(Section IV, Chapters 9, 10, 11, 12)

List below those ideas you identified for specific attention in your coordinated life plan. Add others that may have occurred to you since.

_____
_____
_____
_____
_____
_____
_____
_____
_____
_____
_____
_____
_____

Checkpoint 4: Your Productivity
(Section V, Chapters 13, 14, 15)

List below those ideas you identified for specific attention in your coordinated life plan. Add others that may have occurred to you since.

_____
_____
_____
_____
_____
_____
_____
_____
_____
_____
_____
_____

As you review your summary of the four checkpoints, look for consistencies and inconsistencies. In particular, look for connections between your weak points and your goals. In general, an identified problem will correlate with a goal. In fact, part of the solution may already be indicated. For example, a low-energy-level problem, which relates to inefficient time control, suggests the adoption of some of the time control techniques suggested in Chapter 14 of this book.

Step Two: Summarizing Your Goals

You are now ready to organize your goals into six key categories:

Career
Family
Health
Finances
Personality
Leisure and recreation

The planning strategy charts on the following pages will help you summarize your goals. In the first column on each chart, list your major goals in a particular category. Next, indicate the time frame for each goal (immediate, intermediate, or long-term), keeping in mind that a goal can have both immediate and longer-term elements. In the last column, rank your goals in their order of importance to you, beginning with 1 as your top priority. Check off the two or three goals that you consider the most urgent.

CAREER STRATEGY CHART

STATEMENT OF GOAL	TIME			PRIORITY
	IMMEDIATE	2-5 YEARS	LONG TERM	
1				
2				
3				
4				
5				
6				

FAMILY STRATEGY CHART

STATEMENT OF GOAL	TIME			PRIORITY
	IMMEDIATE	2-5 YEARS	LONG TERM	
1				
2				
3				
4				
5				
6				

HEALTH STRATEGY CHART

STATEMENT OF GOAL	TIME			PRIORITY
	IMMEDIATE	2-5 YEARS	LONG TERM	
1				
2				
3				
4				
5				
6				

FINANCIAL STRATEGY CHART

STATEMENT OF GOAL	TIME			PRIORITY
	IMMEDIATE	2-5 YEARS	LONG TERM	
1				
2				
3				
4				
5				
6				

PERSONALITY STRATEGY CHART

STATEMENT OF GOAL	TIME			PRIORITY
	IMMEDIATE	2-5 YEARS	LONG TERM	
1				
2				
3				
4				
5				
6				

LEISURE AND RECREATION STRATEGY CHART

STATEMENT OF GOAL	TIME			PRIORITY
	IMMEDIATE	2-5 YEARS	LONG TERM	
1				
2				
3				
4				
5				
6				

Step Three: Setting Your Priorities

At this point you are ready to consolidate your top-priority goals under each category. On the chart that follows, list your most important goals from each category—goals that you intend to pursue *right now*. Certainly the ones you checked as "urgent" will be included. Test your top-priority goals in each category in relation to each other and to your overall needs: Are your goals compatible?

PRIORITIES CHART

RANK*	CAREER	FAMILY	HEALTH	PERSONALITY	FINANCES	LEISURE AND RECREATION	RANK
1							1
2							2
3							3
4							4
5							5
6							6
7							7
8							8

*Priority rank established on preceeding charts.

Step Four: Coordinating Your Priorities

Your final task is to establish *overall* priorities for your goals. For example, your number-one career goal is probably more important than your number-one recreational goal. Review and rework your priorities chart several times until the final priorities emerge. However, remember that you want balance. You will concentrate on key goals, but you will also be pursuing other ones simultaneously. For instance, you may decide to read one "fun" book a month or attend a play or concert in addition to other activities. Don't let those goals get lost. List your coordinated priorities on the following chart.

COORDINATED PRIORITIES CHART

PRIORITY	GOAL	CATEGORY (CAREER, FAMILY, ETC.)
1		
2		
3		
4		
5		
6		
7		
8		
9		
10		

PRIORITY	GOAL	CATEGORY
11		
12		
13		
14		
15		
16		
17		
18		
19		
20		

17. Creating an Action Plan

The key to coordinating your mission and the goals that support them is, of course, planning. In earlier sections of this book, you built the foundation for your personal life plan. You established your mission and set priorities for your goals. The final step is to create the action plan that will convert your goals into the activities necessary to achieve them.

Charting Your Action Plan

Probably the best step you can take toward achieving a goal is to plot its accomplishment in chart form. The charts on the following pages were designed for this purpose. A sample chart is shown along with several blank charts for your use. After you have reviewed the sample, develop an action plan for your top-priority goal in each major category.

1. In the top box write down your major goal in a given category (career, finances, and so on). Make sure your statement of the goal is clear and realistic. Under the goal statement indicate a target date—the time you believe you will need to achieve the goal (and the time you are prepared to commit to it). Alongside the goal statement, summarize all the obstacles you can think of that stand in the way of your goal. These will have to be overcome if you are to get where you want to be.

2. In the lower set of boxes, find the subgoal or subgoals that will take you toward your major goal. Perhaps there is only one; more likely there are several. Under each subgoal indicate the time you plan to allocate to it.

3. Analyze each subgoal you identified, and identify the specific steps (activities) needed to achieve it. List these activities alongside the subgoal.

GOAL:

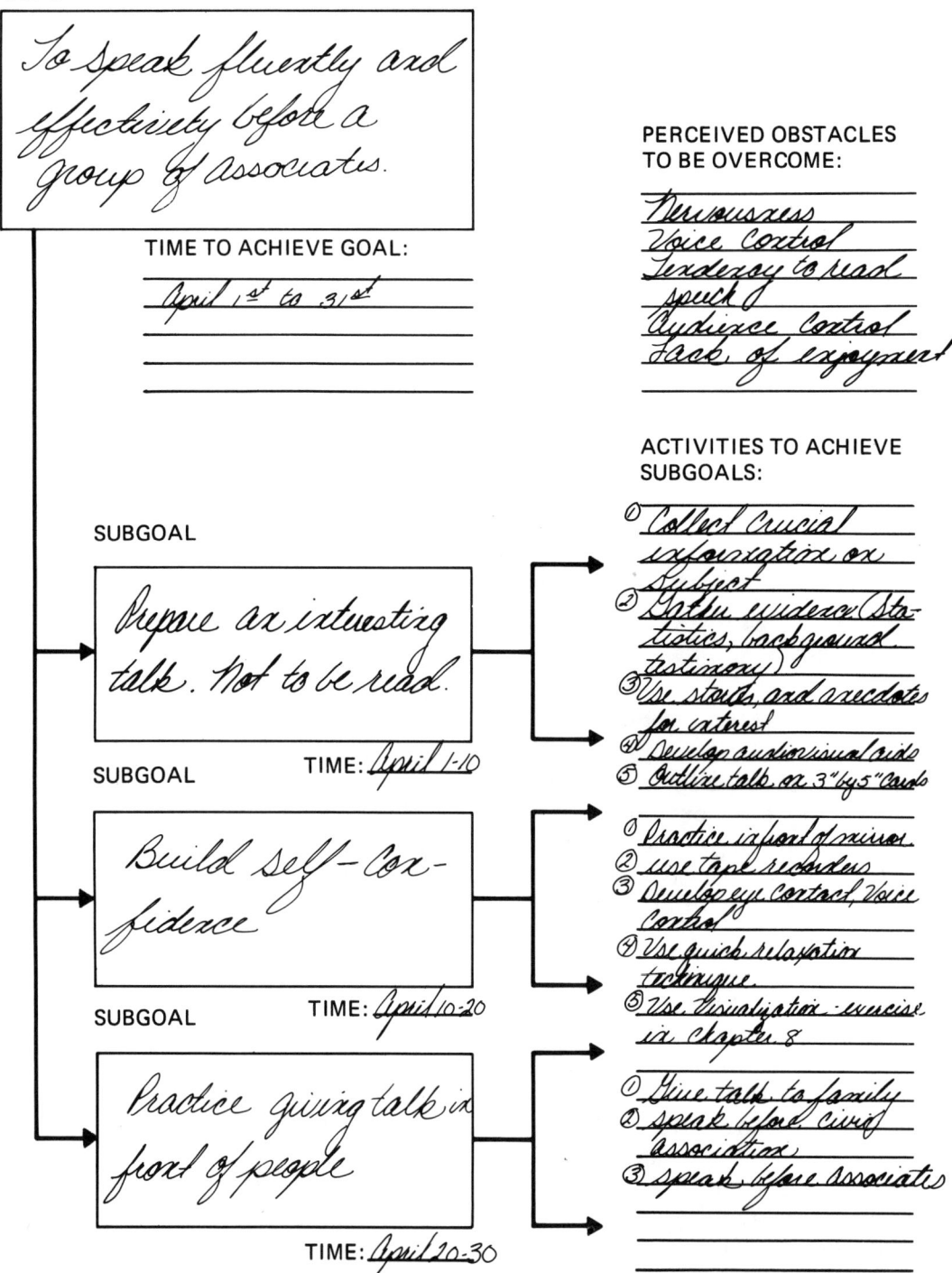

To speak fluently and effectively before a group of associates.

TIME TO ACHIEVE GOAL:

April 1st to 31st

PERCEIVED OBSTACLES TO BE OVERCOME:

Nervousness
Voice Control
Tendency to read speech
Audience Control
Lack of enjoyment

ACTIVITIES TO ACHIEVE SUBGOALS:

① Collect crucial information on subject
② Gather evidence (Statistics, background, testimony)
③ Use stories and anecdotes for interest
④ Develop audiovisual aids
⑤ Outline talk on 3"by 5" cards

SUBGOAL

Prepare an interesting talk. Not to be read.

TIME: April 1-10

① Practice in front of mirror
② Use tape recorders
③ Develop eye contact, voice control
④ Use quick relaxation technique.
⑤ Use visualization exercise in chapter 8

SUBGOAL

Build self-confidence

TIME: April 10-20

① Give talk to family
② Speak before civic association
③ Speak before associates

SUBGOAL

Practice giving talk in front of people

TIME: April 20-30

GOAL: CAREER

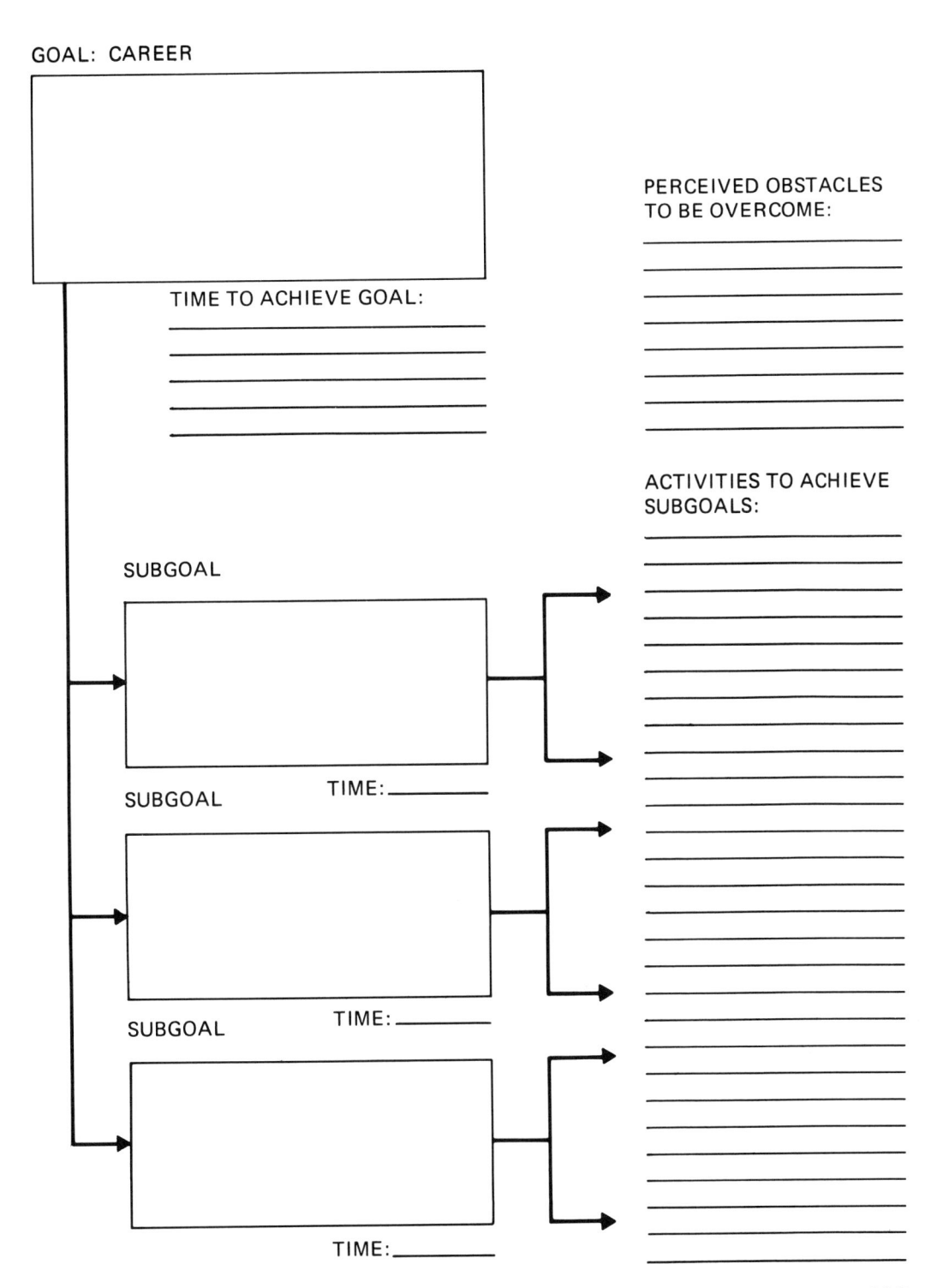

TIME TO ACHIEVE GOAL:
_____
_____
_____
_____
_____

PERCEIVED OBSTACLES
TO BE OVERCOME:
_____
_____
_____
_____
_____
_____
_____
_____

ACTIVITIES TO ACHIEVE
SUBGOALS:
_____
_____
_____
_____
_____
_____
_____
_____
_____
_____
_____
_____
_____
_____
_____
_____
_____
_____
_____
_____
_____
_____
_____
_____
_____
_____
_____
_____
_____

SUBGOAL

TIME: _____

SUBGOAL

TIME: _____

SUBGOAL

TIME: _____

GOAL: FAMILY DEVELOPMENT

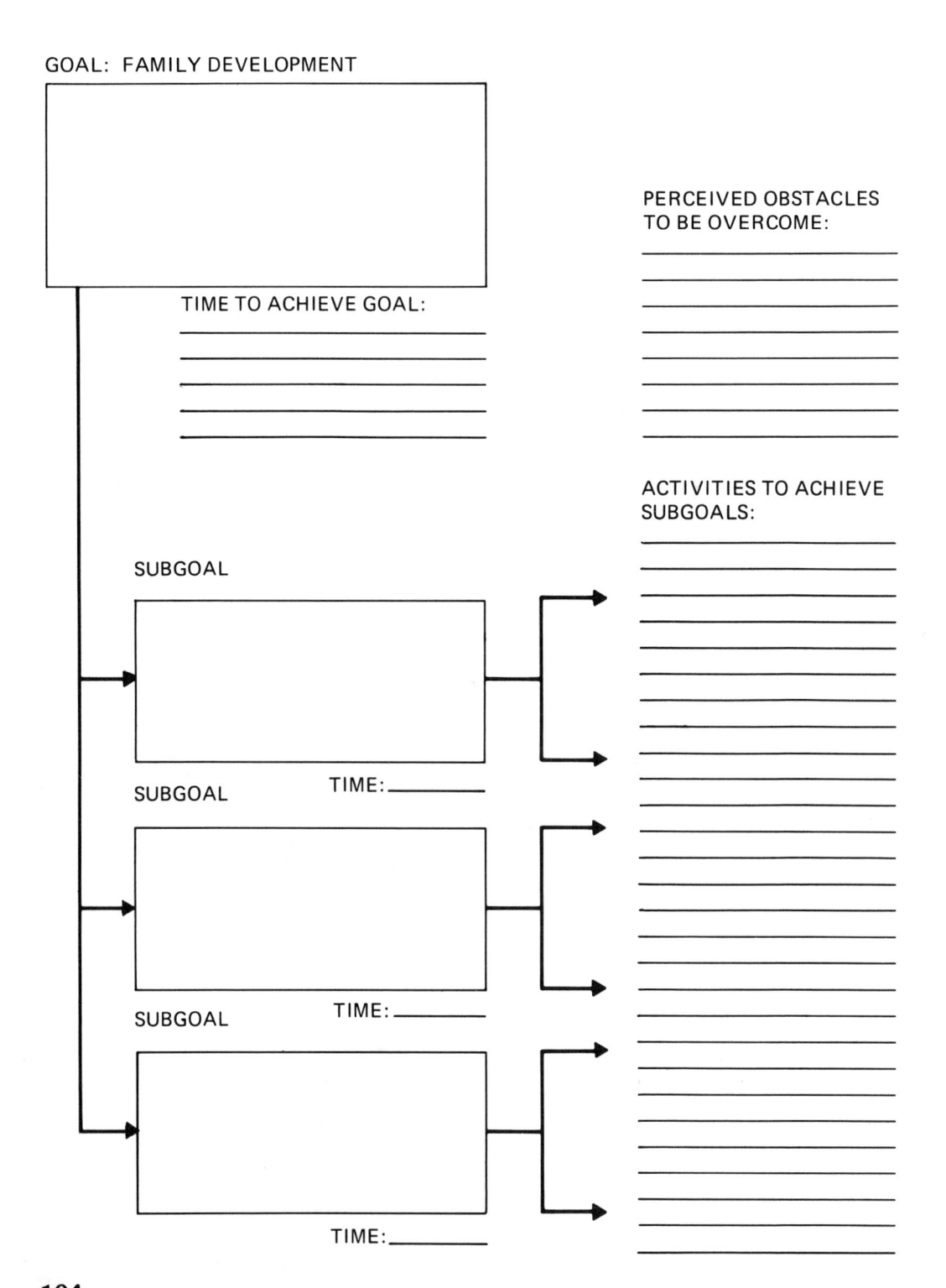

PERCEIVED OBSTACLES
TO BE OVERCOME:

TIME TO ACHIEVE GOAL:

ACTIVITIES TO ACHIEVE
SUBGOALS:

SUBGOAL

TIME: _____

SUBGOAL

TIME: _____

SUBGOAL

TIME: _____

GOAL: HEALTH

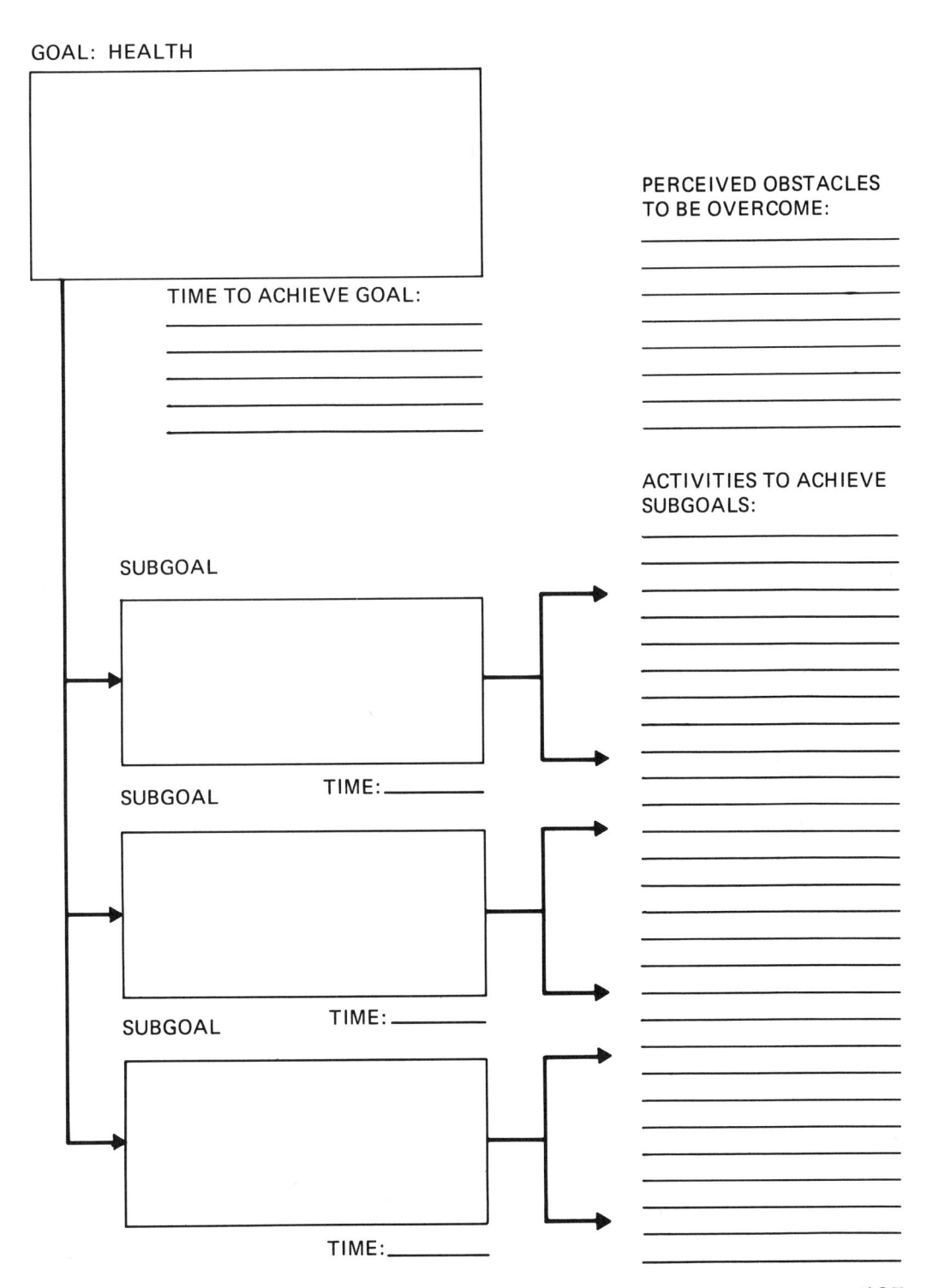

TIME TO ACHIEVE GOAL:
_____
_____
_____
_____
_____

PERCEIVED OBSTACLES
TO BE OVERCOME:
_____
_____
_____
_____
_____
_____
_____
_____

ACTIVITIES TO ACHIEVE
SUBGOALS:
_____
_____
_____
_____
_____
_____
_____
_____
_____
_____
_____
_____
_____
_____
_____
_____
_____
_____
_____
_____
_____
_____
_____
_____
_____
_____
_____
_____

SUBGOAL

TIME:_____

SUBGOAL

TIME:_____

SUBGOAL

TIME:_____

GOAL: FINANCES

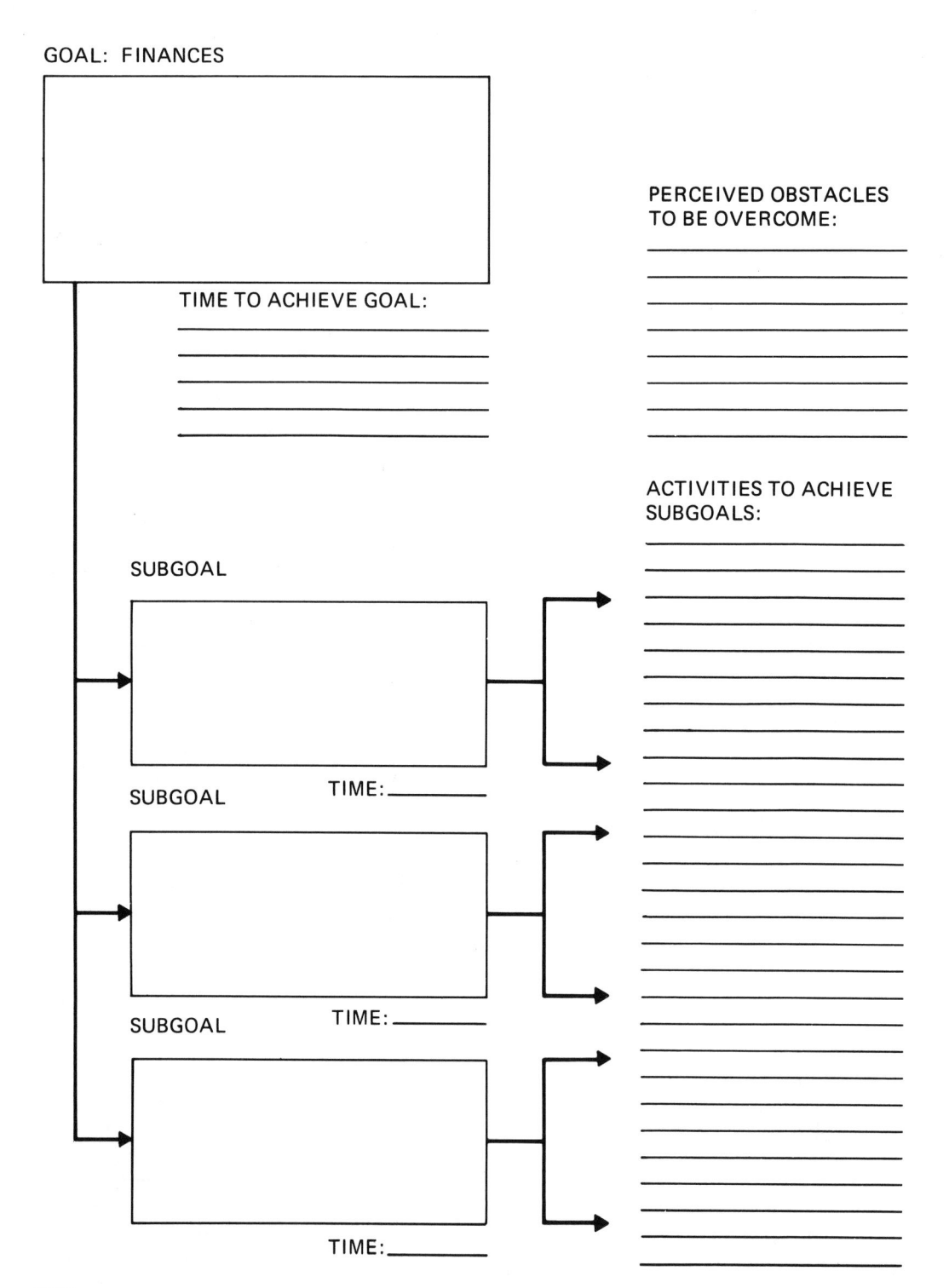

TIME TO ACHIEVE GOAL:

PERCEIVED OBSTACLES
TO BE OVERCOME:

SUBGOAL

TIME: _____

ACTIVITIES TO ACHIEVE
SUBGOALS:

SUBGOAL

TIME: _____

SUBGOAL

TIME: _____

GOAL: PERSONALITY DEVELOPMENT

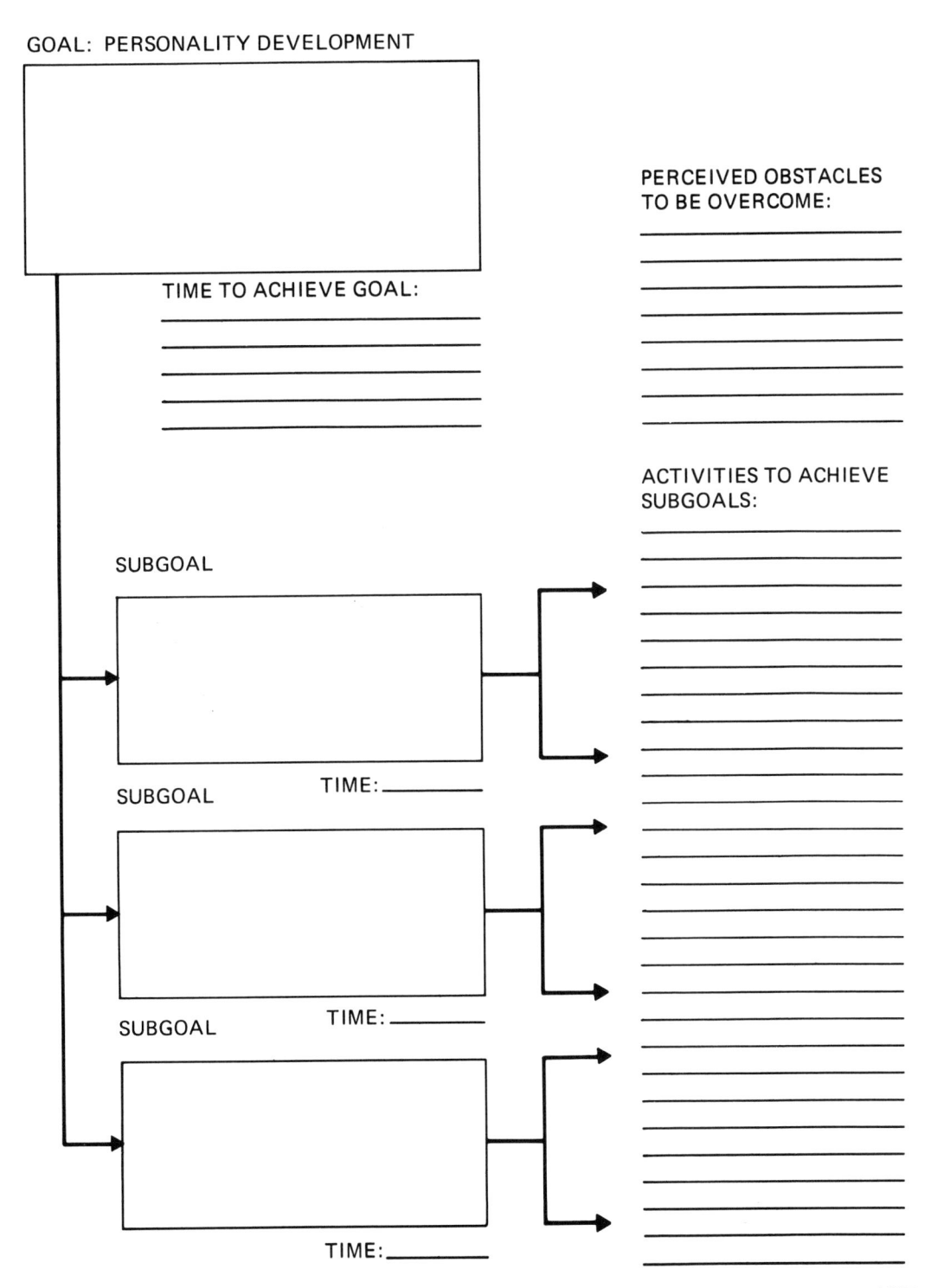

TIME TO ACHIEVE GOAL:

PERCEIVED OBSTACLES
TO BE OVERCOME:

ACTIVITIES TO ACHIEVE
SUBGOALS:

SUBGOAL

TIME: _____

SUBGOAL

TIME: _____

SUBGOAL

TIME: _____

GOAL: LEISURE AND RECREATION

PERCEIVED OBSTACLES
TO BE OVERCOME:
_____
_____
_____
_____
_____
_____
_____
_____

TIME TO ACHIEVE GOAL:
_____
_____
_____
_____
_____

ACTIVITIES TO ACHIEVE
SUBGOALS:
_____
_____
_____
_____
_____
_____
_____
_____
_____
_____
_____
_____
_____
_____
_____
_____
_____
_____
_____
_____
_____
_____
_____
_____
_____
_____
_____
_____

SUBGOAL

TIME: _____

SUBGOAL

TIME: _____

SUBGOAL

TIME: _____

198

Goals and Feedback

In an interview in *Time* magazine, Lee Iacocca, then president of Ford Motor Company, revealed his secret for managing effectively: "At the beginning of every quarter, I sit down with every manager who works for me and we talk about what he is going to produce for us during the coming year. That's his commitment. During the year I help him. At the end of each quarter we sit down and talk about how well he is achieving his goals. At the end of the year we pull out the same memo and talk once more." Every manager at Ford was clear on his goals and knew what was expected of him. He got the help he needed and knew how well he was doing. Good results produced good rewards. Bad results meant being shelved or possibly fired.

This method of management by objectives is highly successful in business. Use it to your own advantage as "self-management by objectives." Give yourself the support that you need and check your progress regularly.

Feedback, of course, is a vital part of your program. It is the measurement of progress toward your goal. It helps you to correct your course and revise your strategies if they are not working. In sports and in other physical activities, feedback is often instantaneous. A baseball pitcher or golfer quickly sees the result of his actions. With career and personal goals, however, results are usually deferred. Such goals may take months or years to achieve.

Because all of us tend to repeat mistakes, it is important that you keep track of where you've been, what mistakes you've made, and how well you are doing in moving toward your goal. You must record your progress. One good way to track your development is to keep a daily journal. Many successful people—Thomas Edison, Albert Einstein, Leonardo Da Vinci—kept a journal or diary of the events of each day. In the journal record your feelings about each day's activities and your progress toward your goals. You might also keep a time log of your activities (see Chapter 14) as well as graphs and charts of your progress.

The action plan progress chart on the following page will help you monitor your achievement and check it against the time you have allocated. If you are not making progress toward your goal, go back and review the steps in your program:

ACTION PLAN PROGRESS CHART

DATE: _____

GOAL	PRIORITY	TARGET DATE	REMARKS

1. Have you clearly defined your goals and subgoals and written them down?
2. Have you fully committed yourself to your goals?
3. Are your goals realistic? Are they manageable? An unrealistic goal can be discouraging; a goal that is too broad can be overwhelming.

Feedback has a strong relationship to your commitment and is a powerful tool in developing potential. Only feedback can help you recognize your success. It pinpoints your gains as well as your errors as you progress toward your goal. Being able to measure your progress is indispensable to success.

Climb Your Mountain!

You've done a lot of reading, soul-searching, and planning up to this point and the time has come to put what you've learned to the test. You're on your own, equipped with a new set of goals and a new outlook on life and on yourself. You've got to follow through to make sure it all falls into place. Here are some key points to remember:

Refer to your "map" at all times. Your map should be a 3" by 5" index card outlining your top-priority goals. They should be clearly defined and realistic, and should have reasonable deadlines. Carry the card with you and read it every day for guidance and inspiration. Remember where it leads—to the top, and to a richer and more rewarding life.

Remember the basics. From your notes, select those exercises and ideas that will help you achieve your goals. Again, write them on 3" by 5" cards and refer to them constantly so that their message becomes engraved in your mind. You will eventually start doing the right things automatically.

Apply yourself with dedication. Since you are the noblest cause ever to come down the pike, how can you help but do your best on your behalf? The keys to your success are commitment, hard work, and discipline. Assault your mountain with enthusiasm and zeal. Support your effort by collecting goal-oriented information from books, seminars, professionals, and other sources. Nourish your commitment with the information you need. Life planning is an ongoing process. Even after you've "arrived" at your goals, you should continue your program to keep yourself in peak shape.

Reinforce your goal-seeking activities. Here's how:

1. Practice the relaxation technique. Visualize what things would be like if you achieved your goals.
2. Develop triggers to elicit certain goal-oriented responses.
3. Remind yourself of your goal. Tape-record your program and play it back daily. Put signs and slogans in your home or office as reminders of your goal.
4. Remember to "role play." Write out your role and make it a part of you.

Measure your progress. For at least a month keep an informal diary of your progress and maintain a time log. Use graphs and other aids to record your progress each week and month in reaching your goal.

Don't rush it. Don't expect immediate results. You cannot predict when the change you want will start to happen. It depends on the nature of your goal. Even if you do your homework, as outlined in the sections on the checkpoints of potential, it may be several months before you start to see significant changes. Many people give up too soon, particularly if they have poor habits that are deeply ingrained or if they face an extremely difficult goal.

Repeat, repeat, repeat. Repetition is essential to a life planning program. If you do not review your plans and goals, they will be forgotten. Go over your notes as frequently as possible until they become a part of you. Keep a tape recorder handy. When an important idea occurs to you, think about it in connection with your work, your goals, your life. Think about how you can apply it. Visualize yourself doing it and the payoff. Then dictate your thoughts into the machine. Set aside a short period each day to listen to what you have recorded.

Once you have defined a goal, and your plans to achieve it, act! Put it to work in your everyday life.

A life which does not go into action is a failure; and this is just as true of a prophet's, a poet's, or a scholar's life as it is true of the life of a man of action.

—Arnold J. Toynbee

One final point. Goal setting is not a static process. Plans change. Circumstances change. Indeed, you will change as you adopt behaviors that help you achieve your goals. Don't let the process grow stale. Review your life plan at least once a year. Identify new priorities and set new goals. As a subgoal becomes a habit (exercise becomes a "way of life" for you, for example), move on to the next one.

Life planning is not a one-shot deal. It is an ongoing process that will help you realize your full potential. So climb your mountain. Start today. Become all that you are capable of becoming!

Index

action plan
   charting, 191–198
   feedback on, 199–201
activity trap, as cause of time mismanagement, 151–152
Alcoholics Anonymous (AA), 72–73
alpha brain waves, 81–82
Anxiety, seriousness of, 27
apathy, cure for, 24

Baruch, Bernard, on love, 41
baseline data, need for, 76–77
Benson, Herbert (*The Relaxation Response*), relaxation technique, 50–51
beta brain waves, 81–82
Body, Mind, and Spirit (Worcester), 27–28
Bok, Edward, on self-worth, 118
Bolles, Richard (*The Three Boxes*), 175
Born to Win (James and Jongeward, 3

career
   development, 119–120
   as dominant structure in life, 34
   evaluating, 108
   potential for growth in, 100–101
   self-image, 100–101
career burnout, 32–33
career indecisiveness, 33–35

checkpoints of potential, 9–12
   coordination of, 11–12
cheerleading, as self-image strengthening technique, 114
"comfort zone" performance level, 64
commitment
   building, 144–146
   discipline as ingredient of, 143
   hard work as ingredient of, 142–143
   importance of, in career, 142
   importance of, in change, 17
   need for, 139
   practical ways to increase, 147–148
   talent as element of, 143–144
   total, 140
communication
   empathy as skill of, 129–130
   golden rule of, 125–126
   importance of, 125
   listening as skill of, 127–128
   paraphrasing as skill of, 128
concentration
   as element of focusing, 30
   value of, 158–159
confidence, 17
   see also self-confidence
coordinated goals statement, 154
coordinated planning, 173–175
coordination, 8
coordination of financial assets, 8–9

coordination of personal assets, 53
Cousins, Norman (*Anatomy of an Illness*), and positive chemical changes, 24
Cronin, A. J., and determination, 11

daily activities record, 154
delegation, for better use of time, 157–158
delta brain waves, 81–82
depression, overcoming, 25, 28
determination, importance of, for success, 68–69
discipline, as element of commitment, 143

Edison, Thomas, on determination, 68
education, as stage of life, 175–176
80/20 trap, as cause of time mismanagement, 152–153
electroencephalograph, for measuring brain waves, 81–82
empathy, importance of, in communication, 129–130
energy
  effect of emotions on, 161–162
  importance of physical fitness for, 164–165
  and negativism, 162
  nutrition as source of, 163
enthusiasm, effect on success, 24
estate planning, 8–9
excellence, desire for, 141
exercise
  importance of, to life, 165–166
  as tension reliever, 52

family
  evaluation of development in, 120–121

fatigue, emotional origin of, 162
finances
  coordination of assets in, 8–9
  evaluation of development in, 122–123
  see also money
focusing
  of goals, 66–67
  in goal setting, 31, 75
  implications of, 30
  importance of, 29
  as key to purpose in life, 32
Franklin, Ben
  on overcoming bad habits, 150
  on overspending, 117
frequency modification, for goal achievement, 85
Friedman, Meyer (*Type A Behavior and Your Heart*), 42
friends, cultivating, 130–131

Gallwey, W. Timothy (*The Inner Game of Tennis*), on concentration, 30
goals
  challenging, 64
  as checkpoint, 11–12
  clearly defining, 146–147
  defining, 74–75
  focusing, 66–67
  frequency modification to achieve, 85
  importance of, 63
  importance of commitment to, 144
  increasing intensity to achieve, 85
  listing, 86–87
  and purposes, 65
  rehearsing, 147
  reinforcing, 78–79
  scientific approach to, 78
  and self-image, 118–124
  setting, *see* goal setting
  and stress, 52–53
  subgoals and, 77–78

taking stock of, 85–86
  tips from pros on achieving, 65
  use of triggers in achieving, 84–85
  visualizing, 81
  written, 75–76
goal setting
  importance of focusing in, 31
  principles of, 74–78
  purpose of, 73
  realistic, 63–64
Gray, Albert M., on purpose in life, 20–21
Guide to Developing Your Potential (Otto), 66

habits, importance of, in time management, 149–150
hard work, as element of commitment, 142–143
health
  evaluation of, 121
  mental, and PMA, 17
  physical, 17, 39–41
hobbies, as tension relievers, 52
Holmes, Thomas H., and life change stress test, 43–45
"hot beliefs," 22–23
Huebner, Solomon, on coordination of financial assets, 8

Iacocca, Lee, on goals, 199
Inner Game of Tennis, The (Gallwey), 30
intensity, increasing, to achieve goals, 85
interpersonal skills:
  empathy, 129–130
  listening, 127–128
  paraphrasing, 128
interruptions, time cost of, 158

James Muriel (*Born to Win*), 3

James, William
  Gifford lectures of, 48
  on habits, 149–150
  on "hot beliefs," 22
Johnson, Lyndon, and use of empathy, 130
Johnson, Wallace, on written goals, 76
Jongeward, Dorothy (*Born to Win*), 3
Judd, H. Stanley (*Think Rich*), on feeling poor, 116

laughing, as tension reliever, 52
Lederer, William (*The Ugly American*), 163
leisure, as stage of life, 175–176
leisure and recreation, evaluation of, 123–124
life change stress test, 43–45
Linkletter, Art (*Yes You Can*), on achieving life goals, 65
listening, importance of, in communication, 127–128

McClelland, David, on reading material, 115
Maltz, Maxwell (*Psycho-Cybernetics*), 48
mental health, importance of positive mental attitude on, 17
mental relaxation, 49–51
Million Dollar Roundtable, 102
mirror technique, to build self-image, 114–115
mission
  defining, 18
  statement, 21–22
money
  and goals, 70–71
  and self-image, 116–117
  see also finances
Monroe, Marilyn, as example of unachieved potential, 106

negativism
  effects of, on life, 18
  as energy stealer, 162
  overcoming, with positive thinking, 28–29
  power of belief against, 26–28
nutrition, and effect on energy, 163–164

Osler, William, on imperturbability, 40
Otto, Herbert A. (*Guide to Developing Your Potential*), 66

paraphrasing, importance of, in communication, 128
Parent, Bernie, and forced career change, 72–73
Patel, Chandra, on stress control, 51
personality, Type A and Type B, 42–43
personality development evaluation, 122
physical appearance, importance of, on self-image, 118
physical conditioning, 165
  see also exercise
physical fitness, effect on energy, 164–165
physical health
  importance of, 17
  and stress, 39–41
physical relaxation, 48–49
planning
  coordinated, 173–175
  coordinating priorities as step in, 189–190
  evaluating checkpoints as step in, 177–179
  setting priorities as step in, 187–188
  sex as factor in, 41
  steps of, 177–190
  as stress reliever, 52–53
  summarizing goals as step in, 180–186
  see also action plan
positive mental attitude (PMA)
  benefits of, 24
  as checkpoint, 11
  dealing with negativism, 26–30
  dealing with stress, 37–55
  developing, 17–18
  importance of, in meeting people, 130
  purpose as factor in, 18–22
positive thinking
  importance of, 17
  steps toward, 28–29
  triggers for, 30
potential
  accurate definition of, 3–5
  for career growth, 100–101
  identified but unused, 6
  pointers for achieving, 4
  quantifying, 13
  unidentified, unrecognized, 6
  use of, 12
power of belief, 26
preoccupation trap, as cause of time mismanagement, 151
pride, 17
priorities
  coordinating, 189–190
  setting, 187–188
productivity
  as checkpoint, 12
Psycho-Cybernetics (Maltz), 48
purpose
  defining, 18
  effect of, on achievement and goals, 65–66
  importance of, 20–21

Rahe, Richard, and life change stress test, 43–45
reading material
  to bolster commitment, 147

effect on self-image, 115
Relaxation Response, The
   (Benson), 50–51
relaxation techniques
   mental, 49–51
   physical, 48–49
   use of, to visualize goals, 82
respect, need for, 23
résumé, use of, to bolster commitment, 147
Rogers, Carl, on empathy, 129
role, defining, 112
role playing, 112–113
Rosenman, Ray H. (*Type A Behavior and Your Heart*), 42
Ross, Leonard, on scientific approach to problem solving, 78

scheduling, for better time management, 157
Scheie, Harold, on getting to the top, 139–140
See You at the Top (Ziglar), 63
self-acceptance, 97–98
self-communication, 125
self-confidence
   as aid in meeting people, 130
   effect of, on self-image, 101–102
   importance of, 80
   testing, 103
self-esteem
   self-acceptance as key to developing, 98
   rating, 104–106
self-evaluation
   career, 108, 119–120
   family, 120–121
   financial development, 122–123
   health, 108, 121
   leisure and recreation, 123–124
   personality, 122

personal strength, 107–111
self-image
   accurate picture of, 5
   building, 104
   career, 100–101
   causes of, 95
   changing, 113
   as check point, 12
   defining, in terms of external goals, 139
   as greatest treasure, 17
   as impediment to work, 95
   importance of, 96
   positive, importance of job on, 35–36
   realistic, 117–118
self-importance, 102
self-pampering, as tension reliever, 52
self-respect, 23
self-stroking, 115–116
self-talk, 125
Selye, Hans
   on aim in life, 19
   on chemical changes due to tension, 24
   on scars from stress, 40
   on stress reduction techniques, 51
sex, as ease to stress, 41
Shapiro, Albert, on success traits, 70
Smith, Stuart F., and coordination of financial assets, 8
Spahn, Warren, on achieving goals, 65
sports, as tension relievers, 52
stages of life, coordination of, 175–176
strategic life planning
   sex as part of, 41
   and stress, 52–53
   see also planning
stress
   and career burnout, 32

stress *cont.*
  consideration of, in life planning 52–53
  controling, 47–48
  effect of, on health, 39–41
  effect of, on mental attitude, 40
  finding cause of, 39
  and functioning, 38–39
  lack of purpose as cause of, 19
  positive response to, 37
  sex as ease to, 41–42
  stress control record, 53–55
Stress Without Distress (Selye), 51
subgoals, as means to success, 77–78
success
  attitude, 113–114
  as encouragement, 64
  traits common to, 70

taking stock of goals, importance of, 85–86
talent, as element of commitment, 143–144
tension relievers, 52
theta brain waves, 81–82
Think Rich (Judd), 116
Three Boxes, The (Bolles), 175
time
  better management of, 157–159
  and habits, 149–150
  increasing productive, 154
  log, 155–157
  practical tips on management of, 159–160
  traps as causes for mismanagement, 150–154
  wasters, 155, 157
TM (Transcendental Meditation), as relaxation technique, 50
"to do" list, usefulness of, 154
Transcendental Meditation (TM). as relaxation technique, 50
triggers, to boost goal achievement, 84–85
Type A and Type B personalities, 42–43
Type A Behavior and Your Heart (Meyer and Rosenman), 42

Ugly American, The (Lederer), 163
U.S. Senate report on dietary habits, 163

values, and self image, 118
visualization of goals
  and role playing, 82–84
  steps in process of, 81
  use of relaxation for, 82

walking, as most efficient form of exercise, 165
Worcester, Elwood (*Body, Mind, and Spirit*), on positive thinking, 27–28
work
  love of, 33, 34
  as stage of life, 175–176
  unhappiness in, 32–33
  see also career
written goals, importance of, 76–77

Zalesnik, Abraham, motivational study of, 5–6
Ziglar, Zig (*See You at the Top*), risks of goal setting, 63

Suggestion Box

To: *How to Get to the Top*
    930 Montgomery Ave., Box 502
    Rosemont, PA 19010

I have the following suggestions for the next edition.

_____
_____
_____
_____
_____
_____
_____
_____
_____
_____
_____
_____
_____
_____

                Name:
                Address: